Editor
Sara Connolly

Cover Artist
Brenda DiAntonis

Editor in Chief
Ina Massler Levin, M.A.

Creative Director
Karen J. Goldfluss, M.S. Ed.

Imaging
James Edward Grace
Ariyanna Simien

Publisher
Mary D. Smith, M.S. Ed.

USING GOOGLE
and Google™ Tools in the Classroom
Grades 5 & Up

D0599183

Author

Midge Frazel, M. Ed.

Teacher Created Resources, Inc.
6421 Industry Way
Westminster, CA 92683
www.teachercreated.com
ISBN: 978-1-4206-2222-5

© 2009 Teacher Created Resources, Inc.
Made in U.S.A.

Teacher Created Resources

Table of Contents

About This Book

Whether you are a classroom teacher, a specialist teacher, a technology facilitator, a curriculum specialist, an administrator, or a college professor, you are a person who works in the field of education and has the need to use the Web and technology tools in your everyday work. An educator is a person who values time and never has enough of it. This book is not the ordinary book that you will find on the shelves of a bookstore in the section marked "Computer Books." Those books are so numerous in pages that it takes an entire week to read the first chapter and are often written specifically for business.

Google™ and Google™ Tools in the Classroom is a practical introduction to what the Google search engine can do for you as an educator, where to find specific Google online applications, and how to use Google Tools in your classroom, office, or lab. In some cases, example lessons are provided to help you get started right away.

The maximum benefit of this book can be made by working with it while you are connected to the Internet and are seated in front of your desktop computer or laptop. In most cases, it will be useable for anyone using a Windows, Macintosh, or Linux-based computer. The best source of help beyond this book is using the support or FAQs (frequently asked questions) areas of Google.

List of Standards-Based Lessons

Throughout the pages of this book, you will find ten standards-based example lessons using some of the newer features of Google Tools. In addition to these, the search techniques offered in the last section of the book can assist you in finding other lessons revolving around Google applications that are on webpages outside of Google. In addition, there are "getting started" ideas to help you design your own lessons with these new tools and applications.

Introduction

What is Google?

Google started out as just a search tool. At the time, there were many search tools found on the Internet. Some were subject-specific directories that had taken webpages on a topic and organized them into something that resembled a card catalog database. Many of these still exist today and are very useful for education. Search engines, on the other hand, allow for searching millions (perhaps trillions) of text keywords and image names on webpages that are gathered in a frequently changing central database housed at the company. This makes it difficult to find specific information about education related topics.

Google is a company that offers both a topic-specific directory and a search engine as its business. As more and more people turn to the Internet for information, the people at Google are constantly looking for new ways to bring the information and content that you need directly to your computer.

The Google Company building is located in Mountain View, California and there are additional locations in many other countries. If you are curious about this, you can find out about it.

Point your browser to:
http://www.google.com/about.html

It is highly unlikely that you have never heard of or used Google, but you may not know about all the new "tools" or applications that Google offers for FREE that are of high interest to educators. Those exciting tools will be the focus of this book and we hope you enjoy learning about them and using them in your classroom. Schools in the twenty-first century have moved far beyond the "talk and chalk" of past generations.

Even by the time you read these words, Google will have developed new tools not covered in this book, or deleted some of the current tools. This is the way of the rapidly changing face of technology.

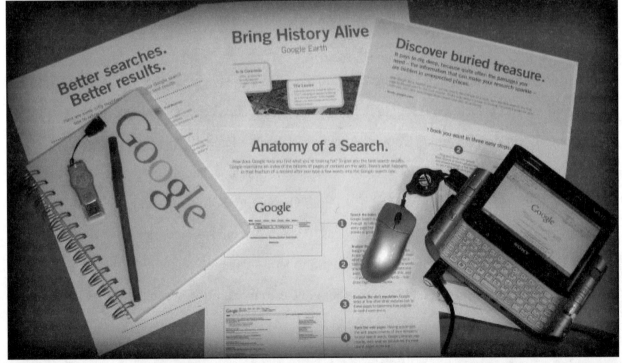

Introduction (cont.)

What are Google Tools?

Google Tools is a catch-all phrase for all the applications that Google has developed or has under development. The most popular tools are Google Docs™, Google™ Earth, Blogger™ web publishing service, Picasa™, Google Notebook™, Google™ Video, and YouTube™, but there are others to explore.

> To see a list, point your browser to:
> **http://www.google.com/intl/en/options/**

Most tools are designed to be used while you are online. This simply means that you use your browser to move to the webpage Google has assigned to them with a regular URL, read the directions, and then use your Google Account to sign in and use the tools.

Some of the Google Tools are collaborative. For example, you can use the Google Docs™ application to create a shared word processing document, spreadsheet, or presentation. All of the people working on the document will need to have a Google Account. It is important to set one up right away.

Setting up a Google Account

A Google Account is different than a Gmail™ webmail service account. If you have a Gmail™ webmail service account, you can use that to set up your Google Account. Setting up a Google Account requires you to have a current email address. Google will send a confirming email to that address after you set up the account. Your Google Account will be used to sign in to Google in order to use the Google Tools. It is important for teachers who are using this book to have a Google Account.

Windows and Macintosh users will need:
- Internet access and a web browser

- An email address (school, personal or Gmail webmail account)

> Point your browser to:
> **http://www.google.com/accounts/NewAccount**

Follow the directions on this page to enter your email address and to choose a password. You will need to confirm your password and then type the word verification characters. (This is to ensure you are not a spammer.) If you are using a school computer, protect your privacy by un-checking the boxes for:

- Remember me on this computer

- Enable Web history

Introduction *(cont.)*

Setting up a Google Account *(cont.)*

Read the Terms of Service and click the Accept button to be on your way.

> If you need help understanding this process, point your browser to:
> **http://www.google.com/support/accounts/**

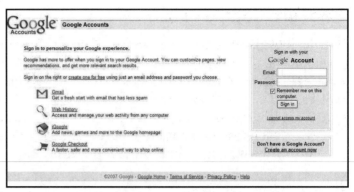

Using your Google™ Account

During the course of learning with this book, you will be using your Google Account to set up and work with the various applications and tools offered by Google. When you wish to access them, simply sign in to your Google Account. When you are signed-in, you will see a link at the top of the Google Search page, or iGoogle™ page, that reads, "My Account." When you click on that link, it will bring you to your account page. On the right hand side of this page you will see a list of your Google Tools. Clicking on a tool will open it so that you can work with it again.

It is important for you to remember to sign out of your Google Account when you have finished working when you are using a shared computer. This ensures your privacy.

What is Google Labs™ Research Division?

Like the science classroom in your school, Google Labs™ research division is the area of Google where you can learn about all of the tools that are currently under development. The best news is that you get to try them out before they are considered "graduates."

> Point your browser to:
> **http://labs.google.com/**

You may see the word "beta" on some of the Google Tools. This is a term used to indicate that the application is still under development and that some of the features may act a bit "flaky" or change over time, just like real science experiments. You can learn more about this by reading about the Google Labs research division.

> Point your browser to:
> **http://labs.google.com/faq.html**

You Tube™ and Google™ Video

Posting video clips to the Web used to be difficult to do until the people at YouTube showed us how and provided the space on their servers at no cost. Video files can be humungous in size! Because of the questionable content of many videos, most schools have their content filtering set to block YouTube, Google Video, and other video websites. Because of this, teachers wishing to view video will have to do so from their home computers. Some video content created is well worth viewing and the medium makes learning faster, easier, and entertaining. Don't just dismiss this just because you can't view it at school.

It is imperative that all videos to be used in the classroom with students are previewed first for appropriate content and connection to the curriculum.

Use Google™ Video video search to find video content hosted either on the Web or by Google. These videos are international in nature and can be politically or sexually controversial. There is a wide range of content for educators to choose from and the best videos are tutorial in nature, explaining in a visual format the newer technologies of the Internet. The future of learning lies in video format.

> Point your browser to:
> **http://video.google.com**

YouTube is the Google tool that you use to post your own videos. You must create an account in order to post videos, but an account is not needed to just view video content. There a limit to the length of the video and the size of the video file that you can post. Read the directions carefully before you create a video. Many educators create a video eportfolio of their work and post it online. There are many excellent, short training videos on topics of interest to educators at the K-12 Education Channel.

> Point your browser to:
> **http://youtube.com**

Some Examples:

> YouTube K-12 Education Channel
> Point your browser to:
> **http://www.youtube.com/group/K12**

> The Google™ Channel
> Point your browser to:
> **http://www.youtube.com/user/Google**

Look for titles such as "Google Apps Team Edition," "Blogger: How to Start a Blog," and "Travel with Google Maps" as examples of what the people at Google have created to help you learn using short video tutorials.

Introduction *(cont.)*

You Tube™ and Google™ Video *(cont.)*

Wes Fryer's Channel
Point your browser to:
http://www.youtube.com/wfryer

Wes Fryer's educational presentations, blog, and podcasts about the Internet and the future of education are a must-see for those who are involved in the changing landscape of education. Wes does a wonderful job at explaining difficult concepts to all educators.

How to Use This Book

In many sections, you will notice a word or series of words next to text that reads, "Google Search Term." These single or multiple words are keywords that you can type into the Google Basic Search page. The resulting hits that appear after you click the Google Search button, will lead you to a page that contains the Google Tool for that section without you having to type the URL that appears in that section.

Google Search term:
Google Patent Search
[or point your browser to: **http://www.google.com/patents**]

In this example, go to the Google Basic Search page and in the search box, type "Google Patent Search" and click the Google Search button. This will bring you to the results page, where the top result shows the link for the URL of **http://www.google.com/patents.** Simply click on the link, and you'll be there without the process of typing that URL!

Google | Google Patent Search | Search

Web

Google Patent Search
Google Patents. Patent Search. BETA. Advanced Patent Search - Google Patent Search Help. Search over 7 million patents. ...
www.google.com/patents - 10k - Cached - Similar pages

Search Tools by Google

To search or to browse; that's the question! With the Web so easy to navigate and filled with more than just static text, people everywhere spend an amazing part of their days clicking from one Web address to the next. But is that an efficient way to find what you are looking for? If you answered "probably not," you were correct. Most users, including educators, have their favorite websites saved to their browsers, and rely mostly on their content. Over time, websites disappear or new curriculum content must be found and this is when educators realize that they need to learn effective search techniques.

The first step in learning to search is knowing the difference between browsing and searching. Browsing is useful if you are familiar with a topic and want to see what other topics might be related or of interest to yours. For this, a subject directory is a good place to start. A subject directory is an organized and usually annotated list of links placed together in a thematic or subject specific manner. An analogy to a subject directory is that it is like a library; purposefully organized by people for easy location of materials. Librarians organize the books so that you can walk to a subject and find a book easily and browse around looking for others on the same topic. In this way, Google's Directory is similar as the links there are selected and organized by people. A directory helps you narrow down your search from a broad topic.

Educators rely on Kathy Schrock's Guide for Educators (**http://school.discoveryeducation.com/ schrockguide**) as the most popular researched and evaluated educational directory on the Web. Teachers with minimal time available to them should look here first to see if Kathy has already included sources on their chosen topic.

A Google Account and a Gmail webmail service account are not required to use Google's Directory.

Windows and Macintosh users will need:
  • Internet access and the use of a web browser (such as *Internet Explorer* or *Firefox*)

Browsing the Directory

Google search term:
Google Directory [or point your browser to http://directory.google.com]

Google Directory Help:
http://www.google.com/dirhelp.html

Google Guide: Directory: Category of Topics
http://www.googleguide.com/directory.html

Search Tools by Google *(cont.)*

Examining the webpage for Google Directory™ web directory, you will see a search box where you can enter keywords and then click the "Search Directory" button. Notice that this button reads "Search Directory" as opposed to the button on Google's main page that reads "Search." It must be emphasized here that Google Directory™ web directory ONLY searches the directory and not the whole Web. Underneath the search box, there is a list of categories of topics and underneath that there are subheadings. The subheadings are there to help you locate a more specific topic within that category.

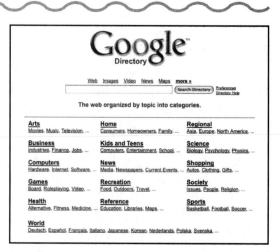

Practice by choosing a category such as "Reference." When you click on it, the page displays all the topics. In alphabetical order, these subcategories are shown with a number in parentheses. For example, click on "Books" and then "E-Books" to see categories of books in electronic format. From there, clicking on "Titles" will bring up more categories of e-books. This process is time-consuming but it does show you the subdivision of materials in the electronic book topics. You may have thought that e-books were something you read on a handheld device but didn't know that many websites contain selected chapters, excerpts, or whole books as an online reading experience.

The Google Directory™ web directory Help page offers more information on how to use the directory. On that page is an explanation of the category "World." This special category in Google Directory™ web directory brings you to directory content in languages other than English. This is useful for teachers of foreign languages and for locating webpages that have been written in another language (not ones translated by the Google™ Language Tools).

Working with Students

Experts agree that students under grade five should only be working with websites that have been specifically identified and evaluated by their teachers. They should not search the Web alone. After this age, student searching techniques should be taught with examples, and results discussed in class. Student evaluation of content of websites should begin as soon as the search techniques lessons are complete. Searching and evaluating are linked without question whether by students or by adults. Teachers need to be skilled in both areas and be knowledgeable about their school district's acceptable use (AUP) policies.

SafeSearch

Google offers a "safe search" feature on its preferences page. For filtering out sexual content, there are two choices available—"strict" and "moderate." "Strict" offers the most control as it filters both text and images while "moderate" filters images only. Click on the link "Preferences" and look for "SafeSearch Filtering." No filtering tool is 100% accurate.

Search Tools by Google *(cont.)*

Searching the Web

Google offers two distinctly different pages for general searching of the vast resources of the Web: "Basic Search" and "Advanced Search." As you learn more about search techniques, you will find yourself using the advanced page more and more as it offers a fast and comprehensive way to find what you are seeking. Taking the time to learn this is essential for all educators and their students. But since many users don't know that the Advanced Search page exists, it is important to look at the Basic Search page first as a place to start thinking about keywords and search terms. To do that you need to know a little bit more about why searching and browsing are different.

Spiders, Crawlers, and Bots

Human beings (that's you!) place the links in the subject directory like Google Directory™ web directory, but they do not place or organize the links that you see when you are using a search engine. Instead, humans write a special mathematical algorithm (or set of rules) that is sent out to the Web to find and bring back information to be stored in the servers at Google. Because this process is ongoing, results can differ each time you enter a search at Google Web Search™ features. This process of entering keywords and terms is called a *query* (like a question). To understand more about this, take a look at the picture on the following webpage.

> How Does a Search Engine Work?
> **http://www.midgefrazel.net/search_slide.htm**

Keywords and Search Terms

All searches must begin with thinking about the words that you type into the search box. A single word or group of words typed in will result in "hits," which are the results you see in the listing. Just like asking the right questions to find out information from another human being, your search results will be better if you think beforehand about what information you expect to find. Search engine queries have been getting better and easier over the years but, like your third grade teacher informed you, "Spelling counts!" as many words in the English language have different spellings for different meanings.

Also, important to know is that Google's results are not case-sensitive so you never need to bother to capitalize any words. But if you do, that's okay as the results will not be different. It will be harder for students to "unlearn" noncapitalization if they don't use capitalization rules every day.

Brainstorming for appropriate keywords and search terms with students is important as they will almost always tell you that the first result at the top of the page is the one you want. They have probably investigated the "I'm Feeling Lucky" link and decided that they have spent enough time searching and this one result will satisfy their quest for answers to their homework assignment. Many times this top link will lead students to Wikipedia, the online encyclopedia which is created completely by users and may not contain correct information as it is not like a print encyclopedia in which the content is edited by experts. Don't believe everything you read on the Web!

Search Tools by Google *(cont.)*

To learn more about keywords, read the information at this website:

> The Spider's Apprentice
> **http://www.monash.com/spidap.html**

Google™ Basic Search

Google's Basic Search page is uncluttered and simple to use. It contains a search box where you can type in a word or few words before you click the Google Search Button or press the Enter or the Return key on your keyboard.

> Google search term:
> **Google** [or point your browser to **http://www.google.com**]

Let's imagine you have seen or read something about WebQuests, which are a popular critical-thinking Web based project created by teachers for students, but you don't know how to find out more about them. Using Google's Basic Search page, type the keyword "webquest" into the search box and click the Google Search button.

Examine the results. The information bar just above the hits tells us that Google has found over a million webpages that contain the single word "webquest" and is displaying them ten links at a time. It would take quite a while to go through these results. In this case, the first result is the one you would want to use to begin learning about this valuable classroom project. Google results give you valuable information about the "hit" even before you click on the link to move to that webpage.

Below the "hit" link, is a partial description of the webpage, usually written by the person who authored this particular webpage. This information is followed by another line with the web address (in this case webquest.org), the size of the page, and a link to the cached page and pages similar to the one you have located. A cached page is a "snapshot in time" of that page. This is useful if there is a problem with that page at the given moment you would like to view it, as perhaps the server holding that page is down for repair. You can at least examine the cached page to see if you need to return to it later. The Similar Pages link produces a list of pages that you may find of interest, mainly ones that have the same keyword.

Search Tools by Google *(cont.)*

Google™ Basic Search *(cont.)*

You may notice that several hit pages include sponsored links, which are paid advertising offered by Google's Ad Words business side. People pay for Google to post these links at the top or the side of the hit results. This is one way that Google gets paid for providing their search services and applications for free.

> Google's Basic Search Help
> **http://www.google.com/help/basics.html**

Sometimes Google's Basic Search page will look a bit different. Google's official artist, Dennis Hwang, designs special Google Logos for different occasions, and the people at Google set a link for that particular event (usually a day) with a keyword or set of keywords. The logos for these events have been archived from 1999 to the present.

It's Spring!

People are naturally curious about this interesting feature of Google Search and the people at Google have a webpage or two set aside to display these creations. Recently, Google held a design contest for students in schools in the United States so they could join the creative fun in designing their own Google Logos. Even if the contest is over, you can access the information and lessons offered by the education staff for this event.

> Google Holiday Logos
> **http://www.google.com/holidaylogos.html**
>
> Google Fan Logos (created by other artists)
> **http://www.google.com/customlogos.html**
>
> Doodle 4 Google
> **http://www.google.com/doodle4google/**

Search Tools by Google *(cont.)*

Google Advanced Search

Google's Basic Search often returns results with a million or more hits and that number increases with each passing hour. After you and your students become more familiar with brainstorming keywords and reading resulting pages using the basic search, it is time to move forward to learning and using the Advanced Search page.

Google Advanced Search [**http://www.google.com/advanced_search**]
or simply click the "Advanced Search" link on the Basic Search page
Google Advanced Search Help
http://www.google.com/intl/en/help/refinesearch.html

Google Web Search Features
http://www.google.com/help/features.html

Google Support Page
http://www.google.com/support/

Google Guide: "Making Searching Even Easier"
http://www.googleguide.com/

4 NETS for Better Searching
http://webquest.sdsu.edu/searching/fournets.htm

Even though the Advanced Search page of Google is better to understand and use, it is still important to know a little about the "operators" which help you narrow down your searches. This requires a bit of Boolean lingo, which may sound painful but is easy to learn once you've been reintroduced to the vocabulary that you learned back in algebra class.

Hello, Operator?

In the early years of telephones, you had to make a phone call by alerting the operator. Examine the telephones around you. On the button marked with a zero, you might see the letters 'OPER." It's hard to believe it, but before there was 911 service, pressing this button was the only way to get help. Appropriately, this section is about "operators," which are special keywords and symbols that Google's search capabilities provide to perform focused searches, which is not unlike summoning a magic genie. In this case, the genie is named Rockwell and he is a real person.

Point your browser to:
Rockwell Schrock's Excellent Boolean Machine
http://www.kathyschrock.net/rbs3k/boolean/

By using this special Venn diagram, you can hover your mouse over each of the words AND, OR and NOT and read the description under the circles. Keeping this in mind, move to Google's Advanced Search page and try it out.

Search Tools by Google *(cont.)*

Google Advanced Search *(cont.)*

Notice the tip links at the end of the search boxes? Click on each one to see what each box means and compare it to the words you learned using Rockwell's Excellent Boolean Machine.

- ALL the words: the first line search box
- OR either word: the third line search box
- NOT excludes words: the fourth line search box

Now let's say that you are searching for information about endangered birds. As you type words into these boxes, a sample "search expression" appears. The first choice (ALL/AND) in the first line search box is easy to follow as both words *endangered birds* appear. Click the Advanced Search button. Examine the results and return to the advanced page to try another search. You will have to delete the words you typed previously.

The third line choice (OR), in the third line has you typing the word *endangered* in the first box and birds in the second box to create the "search expression" endangered OR birds. Examine the results and return to the advanced page to try another search. You will have to delete the words you typed previously.

The fourth line choice (NOT), requires you type the word *endangered* in the first line box and the word *birds* to create the search expression endangered –birds. Notice that there is a space between the word *endangered* and the *minus (sign) birds*. Examine the results, noticing that some of the hits have nothing to do with birds, and then return to the advanced page to try another search. You will have to delete the words you typed previously.

Phrase Searching

The second line search box is a special situation and will be very useful to you. Phrase searching combines two or more words together to find those words next to each other on the webpages of the hits. Phrase searching works miracles for many searchers with other databases too and used to be a big secret with early searchers who wished to narrow down searches quickly. To use phrase searching with Google, you type the words on the second line and click the Advanced Search button.

Phrase searching is different from an "all of the words" search in that the words will have to be found together and not on different parts of the page. In a webpage, which is very long with a lot of text, phrase searching quickly finds words that are together. It should be noted that you can use phrase searching with Google's Basic Search page by enclosing the phrase within quotation marks. You may have noticed that Google's Advanced Search page put the quotation marks around the phrase for you.

Search Tools by Google *(cont.)*

Google Advanced Search *(cont.)*

In the "Need More Tools?" section of the Advanced Search page, Google offers you some choices for this search only. If you would like to see more search results on a page (10, 20, 30, 50 or 100) or to choose a specific language for this search, explore these first two choices.

Of particular interest is the ability to search to locate different file types. Use the dropdown box next to "File type" to see the choices. As an example of the usefulness of this type of search, perhaps you are looking to find posted presentations on the topic of the "Salem Witch Trials" for a social studies or English unit. Changing the file type to .ppt and entering the phrase, "salem witch trials" and then clicking the Advanced Search button will yield several pages of presentations on this topic.

With the popularity of Google Earth's (KMZ) files posted as "tours" on webpages; Web 2.0 tutorials in *Shockwave Flash* (SWF); and handouts, manuals, and lesson plans available in *Adobe Acrobat* (PDF); this "Advanced Search" page can quickly lead you to these files that are not often seen in the first few pages of a search.

Search Tools by Google *(cont.)*

Google Advanced Search *(cont.)*

Searching through a domain name was always a popular method to find information on pages of educational institutions (.edu), but with the explosion of video on the Web in the past few years, being able to search a particular domain like youtube.com has become essential. Users can search an entire domain for documents of a particular file type.

Below this section on the Google Advanced Page is a link that reads, "Date, usage rights, numeric range and more." Notice the plus symbol that precedes this link? It indicates that you can expand the information to show more. Click on the link to see what other search options are available. When you are finished, you can click the link again to close the expansion.

Search Tools by Google *(cont.)*

Google Advanced Search *(cont.)*

Most importantly, this is where you can turn Safe Search on for advanced search. The first choice, date, limits your search from "anytime" to more recent dates in order to eliminate "older" information. "Usage rights" is for locating published information, so click on the "Usage Rights" link for an explanation. If you are looking for sites that offer content that can be legally modified or copied, sites which often display on their webpages a "Creative Commons" license notice, this is a good way to find them quickly. More information for these useful search features are found by clicking the "Advanced Search Links" anytime at the top of Google's Advanced Search Page.

As a final treat, take a look at a tool not developed by Google, which uses the search capabilities of Google. It is useful for finding movies, music, stocks and package tracking numbers which are all things of interest to teachers when they are involved in their life outside of school. Try it!

Soople
http://soople.com/

Google Glossary™ Glossary Service

What is Google Glossary™ glossary service?

Although online dictionaries are plentiful on the Web, it is not always easy to find the right one to define words in all disciplines, especially with arcane words or terms and acronyms that have to do with technology. Google offers a specialized search method which is called "definitions." (Unlike other tools of Google, this is a search technique, not an application, so you will see results that are not hosted by Google.) Definitions for medical conditions, scientific terms, and acronyms may not be in the dictionaries found in the classroom, but are easily looked up via Google. A Google Account or Gmail™ webmail service is not needed to use Google Glossary.

Windows and Macintosh users will need:
  • Internet access and the use of a web browser (such as *Firefox* or *Internet Explorer*)

How do I use Google Glossary™ glossary service?

  • Point your browser to **http://www.google.com**

  • Type the text "define" followed by a space and then the word you are looking up. Then click the Google Search button.

    Example: define copasetic
    Example: define ROFWL

Search Tools by Google *(cont.)*

Google Glossary™ Glossary Service *(cont.)*

Google Web Search Words
http://www.google.com/support/bin/answer.py?answer=50187

When is Google Glossary™ glossary service most useful?

In years past, teachers assigned weekly spelling words and their definitions to students for increased vocabulary skill building. Typically, students completed these assignments using a dictionary from the classroom library or a dictionary in their home. It was a dreaded assignment for many students, and teachers struggled to make this required school assignment a more interesting task by having spelling bees, making creative writing assignments, and by developing lessons where the words and the definitions fit into other subject disciplines. But in today's world, spell-checking with a word processor has changed the way we learn to spell. Teachers face another technological hurdle because students are simply copying and pasting definitions from the online dictionaries into these weekly tasks.

Google Glossary is available from Google SMS by cell phone, a fact that teachers may not be aware of and need to learn about.

When using Google Glossary and associated online dictionaries, elementary and middle school educators should teach a lesson about copyright laws and plagiarism prior to this assignment and look for an online dictionary that offers audio pronunciation of words. Examine the search results for Google Glossary for one of these tools.

Google Weather

What is Google Weather?

Somehow people are only interested in the weather when weather conditions are less than favorable or predicted not to be to their liking. Google's weather data is taken from The Weather Underground. You can add a Weather "gadget" to your iGoogle classroom page for easy access to weather in your school's area or in an area of the United States your class is studying.

A Google Account or Gmail™ webmail service is not needed to use Google Weather unless you are using the gadget in iGoogle.

Search Tools by Google *(cont.)*

Google Weather *(cont.)*

How do I use Google Weather?

From the main search page of Google, type the word weather followed by a space and then the location. You can search by city and state or by zip code. For larger cities, just the city name will do. Currently, this weather search is limited to the United States.

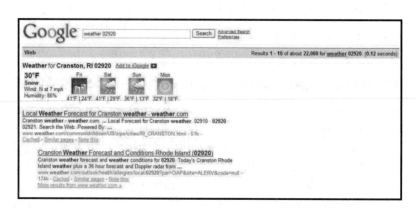

Standards–Based Lesson: Whether Weather is Dangerous?

MCREL Standards

Decision Making: Standard 6: "Applies decision-making techniques": Grades 6-8; Level III, Benchmark 1:1, 1:2, 4:1, 4:2, and Grades 9-12: Level IV, Benchmark 1:2, 5:2

Self-Regulation: Standard 3: "Considers Risks": Grades K-12: Level IV, Benchmark 1:1

1. Instructing students to have an awareness of how dangerous and destructive weather can be fits into teaching the processes of decision-making. Weather can have severe impact on population and the economy. A youthful lifestyle tends to be impulsive and risk-ridden by nature, and students may think of weather as exciting and fun until they experience loss and even death. Promote classroom discussion about emergency preparedness using images of extreme weather from around the country. Have students assemble a list of hazardous weather nationwide (flood, blizzard, tornado, mud slide, ice, hurricane, avalanche) for a discussion on which areas of our country are affected by each of these weather phenomena.

2. Divide the class into the regions of the United States, promoting geography in the classroom. Have each team locate a city within that region, find its zip code, and use Google Weather to track the weather over the course of the project. Older students can use Google Maps™ mapping service to examine the city streets to find out more about the location.

3. Use Google News and Google Images to find photos and information about specific extreme weather conditions that have occurred in the past in that area. Use Google Docs (spreadsheet) to gather the information about temperature highs and lows. Older students can use Google Docs (presentation) to create presentations about the various wild weather events in their region and how the economy is changed after the event is over.

Search Tools by Google *(cont.)*

Google™ Calculator

What Is Google Calculator?

Instead of using a handheld calculator, you can use Google to solve anything from simple addition to complex scientific or mathematical problems. If you are a teacher of consumer and family science, you can use Google Calculator to teach accuracy of measurement in cooking classes.

Teachers of math and science often allow calculator use in the classroom. Using Google for this task means that students do not have to remember to bring their calculators to class. This feature of Google is handy for those classrooms where there is a projection device that can be used in place of a non technology-based whiteboard.

To facilitate the use of this tool, there's a "cheat sheet" to help you get started and two websites to inspire you. A Google Account or Gmail™ webmail service is not needed to use Google Calculator.

Windows and Macintosh users will need:
- Internet access and the use of a web browser (such as *Firefox* or *Internet Explorer)*

How do I use Google Calculator?

1. Point your browser to: **http:// www.google.com**

2. Use the search box to type the mathematical expression you'd like to solve.

3. Press the Enter key on your keyboard or click the Search button.

    Google Calculator Help page
    http://www.google.com/help/calculator.html

    Google Calculator "Cheat Sheet"
    http://www.googleguide.com/help/calculator.html

    Roman Numeral Math
    http://www.education-world.com/a_lesson/02/lp276-03.shtml

    Is it Cold?
    http://www-tcall.tamu.edu/taesp/resources/ged02lesson/18iic.htm

Why should I use Google Calculator?

Using Google as a calculator can enhance lessons that involve Roman numerals, hexadecimal conversion, miles to kilometers, Fahrenheit temperatures to Celsius temperatures, and even some liquid measurement equivalents.

Search Tools by Google *(cont.)*

Google Calculator *(cont.)*

Examples of the Use of Google Calculator

How old are you in seconds?

[type your age and then the words "in seconds"]

Example: 15 years in seconds: 15 years = 473,353,890 seconds

What is your year of birth in Roman numerals?

[type the year and then the words in Roman}

Example: 1985 in Roman numberals: 1985 = MCMLXXXV

This map says it is 45 km to my destination, so how far is that in miles?

[type the number of km and then the words "in miles"]

Example: 45 km in miles: 45 kilometers = 27.9617037 miles

Google Image Search™ Image Search Service

What is Google Image Search?

Digital photography has changed the way that we look at photography. Many digital images are available on the Internet, making learning about copyright laws of great importance. Students are often falsely under the impression that is okay to take any image found on the Web and use it on a webpage, blog, or presentation, even if credit is given. Hotly debated are the "fair-use" rules for using other people's work, including photographs, in education.

On the positive side, it is perfectly legal to examine photographs, diagrams, and illustrations found online and learn from them. For each photograph or image found during a search, be sure to examine the webpage containing the image for copyright restrictions.

A Google Account or Gmail webmail service is not needed to use Google Image Search.

Windows and Macintosh users will need:
- Internet access and the use of a web browser (such as *Firefox* or *Internet Explorer*)

Where is Google Image Search?

Google search term:
Google Image Search [or point your browser to http://images.google.com]

Advanced Image Search
http://www.google.com/advanced_image_search

Google Image Search FAQs
http://images.google.com/help/faq_images.html

Copyright with Cyberbee (Linda C. Joseph)
http://www.cyberbee.com/copyrt.html

Search Tools by Google *(cont.)*

Google Image Search™ Image Search Service *(cont.)*

Who should use Google Image Search?

Educators whose lessons for students require that their students learn about visual literacy should use the search capabilities of Google Image Search to find photographs and images that relate directly to the standards and benchmarks of the lesson. Images in textbooks have long provided students with visual learning but the text in these books encompassed the majority of the material. For those students who are struggling with reading, photographs can be a strong motivator for learning.

Because of the large amount of inappropriate and objectionable images on the Web, teachers using Google Image Search should always have students perform their searches using the filtering of "Safe Search," which is found on the Advanced Image Search page. Teachers should also be observing by monitoring screens while students locate images for the assignment.

Why should we use Google Image Search?

Google Image Search is very useful for finding webpages which may have content which teachers can use to prepare for student instruction. For example, a search using the "Advanced Image Search" in which the keyword phrase "Revolutionary War" is entered in the "Find results related to the exact phrase" box results in images of paintings, cartoons, and maps. There are a surprising number of results, considering that the camera was not invented to take photos during those battles.

Students working with literature studies can use Google Image Search to locate author photographs, as many books in paperback do not include these photographs. They can also search for images related to the books they are reading. As an example, a search for Laura Ingalls Wilder yields interesting photographs of this classic "Little House" fiction series that is widely read in elementary classrooms. In addition to her photograph, there are photographs of places, personal objects, and book covers that make the reading of these Chapter books exciting for younger students.

Search Tools by Google *(cont.)*

iGoogle™ Personalized Search Service

What is iGoogle?

Formerly called "Google™ Personalized Homepage," iGoogle is a way to make a special search page that collects information and displays it all on one page. You design this page yourself by adding pre-created "gadgets" from a list. You can create an iGoogle page with or without signing in to a Google Account or having a Gmail webmail service account.

A "gadget" is the name of a small application that you pick from a list and then chose to add it to your page. They range from the silly to the incredibly useful. When you set up your iGoogle page, several "gadgets" are added automatically to show you what is available.

Where is iGoogle?

Google search term:
iGoogle [or point your browser to **http://www.google.com/ig/**]

iGoogle Info
http://www.google.com/support/bin/topic.py?topic=9003

Directions for using iGoogle with or without a Google Account
http://www.google.com/support/bin/answer.py?answer=25551

Making iGoogle your classroom page (see lesson in this section)
http://www.google.com/support/bin/answer.py?answer=25557&ctx=sibling

Who should use iGoogle?

Classroom teachers who have a single computer in their classroom as a learning center or as a "research" station can set up an iGoogle page and personalize it for the specific needs of the main topic of study. For elementary and middle school students, teachers should select the "gadgets" to be used on the classroom iGoogle page.

Some high-school students can use iGoogle to create gadgets of their own design as a project for computer science classes. All high-school students can use an iGoogle page on their home computer to aid in their knowledge of finding and managing information.

Teachers can assign a student or small group of students to be the "online reporter" of the day and have them summarize and report to the class on what was found on their classroom iGoogle page for the day.

Why should I use iGoogle?

Setting up an iGoogle page on your home computer can help educators keep up with current events, changes in the weather, and managing household dates and "to-dos." For those teachers taking a graduate class, iGoogle can help with managing assignments.

Search Tools by Google *(cont.)*

iGoogle™ Personalized Search Service *(cont.)*

iGoogle should be used to display "gadgets" with content that is constantly changing. Those "gadgets" that are used for display of current news headlines, time, and phases of the moon will change each time the personalized iGoogle page is accessed.

When is iGoogle most useful?

This Google application is most useful when used with faculty or students who are not familiar with using web-based tools. As iGoogle is easy to set up, it is a good first step for people to work with after they get their Google Accounts and want to try out a tool.

Standards–Based Lesson: Creating a Classroom Page with iGoogle

MCREL Standards

Science: Standard 3: "Understands the composition and structure of the universe and the Earth's place in it": Grades 6-8; Level III, Benchmark 3:3

Social Studies: Standard 46: "Understands long-term changes and recurring patterns in world history": Grades 5-6, Level II, Benchmark 46:1. Standard 1: "Understands and knows how to analyze chronological relationships and patterns"; "Grades 6-8, Level 3, Benchmark 2:1

1. Using the Google Search term "iGoogle," move to the starting webpage for this tool. Use the link at the top right of the page to sign in to your Google Account. After signing in you will be brought to the iGoogle start page where you can customize your content with "gadgets."

2. Clear the checkboxes for the suggested gadgets that do not match your curriculum purpose and click the SAVE button. This brings you to a page where you can add your own gadgets by using the "Add Stuff" link. When you find one, click the "Add it Now" button to place it on your page. When you return to your page, you can drag and drop the gadgets around on the page by placing your cursor on the title bar of each one.

3. For this lesson, "Current Moon Phase," "Google Earth: Today's Exploration," and "Google Map Search" have been chosen and matched to the standards listed here, but you should choose ones that meet your curriculum needs as gadget names change and new ones are added frequently. If you have a Google Notebook set up, that can also be added as a gadget.

Search Tools by Google *(cont.)*

iGoogle™ Personalized Search Service *(cont.)*

Standards–Based Lesson: Creating a Classroom Page with iGoogle *(cont.)*

4. To make this your classroom start page, follow the directions given in "Where is iGoogle?" to see this page in your browser. Anytime you wish to return to the regular Google Search page, simply click the link "Classic Home" or type a new URL in the address bar of your web browser.

Specialized Google Tools

Google Web Search™ features several focused search tools separate from the general searching process. These are of high interest to educators because they are a quicker way to find just the right resource. Teachers should know about these focused tools as students will have more need of online resources as they progress through their years in school.

Google Patent Search™ Service

What is Google Patent Search service?

Google's Patent Search is a specialized search tool for finding patents. The patents that you search for are provided by the United States Patent and Trademark Office (USPTO) and therefore are for inventions patented by Americans. A Google Account or Gmail™ webmail service is not needed to use Google Patent Search.

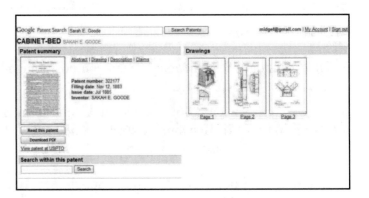

Windows and Macintosh users will need:
Internet access and the use of a web browser (such as *Firefox* or *Internet Explorer*)

Where is Google Patent Search service?

Google search term:
Google Patent Search [or point your browser to **http://www.google.com/patents/**]

About Google's Patent Search
http://www.google.com/googlepatents/about.html#faq

Google Patent Search Help
http://www.google.com/googlepatents/help.html

"What in the World is That?" from the Library of Congress
http://memory.loc.gov/learn/features/science/resources.html

Search Tools by Google *(cont.)*

Google Patent Search™ Service *(cont.)*

Where is Google Patent Search service? *(cont.)*

The First Patent
http://www.me.utexas.edu/~lotario/paynter/hmp/The_First_Patent.html

The Cabinet Bed
http://www.csupomona.edu/~plin/inventors/goode.html

Who should use Google Patent Search service?

Educators who are teaching units that involve invention in United States History or Science will find Google Patent Search easy to use. Providing students with lessons that stimulate curiosity and critical thinking can be easily designed through the study of invention. Using the links provided in this lesson, locate an inventor or invention that connects to your curriculum in history or science.

Why should I use Google Patent Search service?

Digital Citizenship lessons require teachers to have knowledge of intellectual property, copyright, trademarks, and patents. As invention has its successes and failures, students can study the work of the American inventor, Thomas Edison to learn about how science and technology's progress of today is dependent upon Edison's designs of yesterday.

Standards–Based Lesson: What Did Sarah E. Goode Invent?

MCREL Standards

Technology: Standard 3: "Understands the relationships among science, technology, society, and the individual": Grades 3-5: Level II, Benchmark 3:3, 3:4 and Grades 6-8 Level IIII, Benchmark 4:8

1. Point your browser to the page for Google Patent Search. On the main page, five patents are displayed. To change the choices displayed here, simply click the refresh or reload button on your browser. This is a simple way to stimulate curiosity about patents and to explain the process of using this search tool to students. Not all the choices displayed will connect to your lessons, but it is a good way to introduce students to world commerce and economics. When you find a patent you are interested in, click on it to move to that patent page.

2. Using the Google Patents search box, search for the inventor "Sarah E. Goode." This will bring you to the patent page for the Cabinet Bed. Use this patent to show students that each patent has a number assigned to it, and that the dates of filing the patent is different from the date the patent was issued. The patent is available for download as an Adobe Reader document (.pdf) so that students can use it as part of their research projects when they are offline.

Search Tools by Google *(cont.)*

Google Patent Search™ Service *(cont.)*

Standards–Based Lesson: What Did Sarah E. Goode Invent? *(cont.)*

3. As part of a study in the month of March for Women's History Month, encourage students to find out more about Sarah E. Goode. Explain how inventors gain ideas for new inventions from study of older inventions. Ask students to investigate the invention that was invented in 1916 that evolved from the invention by Sarah Goode.

Google Book Search™ Service

What is Google Book Search Service?

Google Book Search™ service is a search tool that searches the full text of the books that Google has digitized and added to its database of titles. Only the books that are considered public domain and copyright free are available for download in PDF format. These books can be printed after downloading if needed. You can create a special library of titles that are of interest, but you must sign in to your Google Account to use this feature.

Google Book Search has an association with *WorldCat* to provide a list of libraries that have the book that you have located in their holdings. Most importantly, it provides an easy citation tool that displays the correct citation in most commonly used formats and for those using the commercial bibliographic tools *EndNote* or *RefWorks*, as the citation can be exported to either of those applications.

You can view selected pages from Google's other books in their database to give you a sample representation of what that book is like. At the Main search page, try moving your mouse, without clicking, over each book cover to see the title, author, and publication date in a bubble. Every time you refresh your browser page, this starting point page changes. The categories include both fiction and nonfiction titles.

Windows and Macintosh users will need:

- Internet access and the use of a web browser (such as *Firefox* or *Internet Explorer*)
- A Google Account (for creating a library of your own)

Web   Images   Maps   News   Shopping   Gmail   more ▼   My library | Sign in

Google™ Book Search BETA   [   ]   (Search Books)   Advanced Book Search
Google Book Search Help

Google has reached a groundbreaking agreement with authors and publishers.

Search Tools by Google *(cont.)*

Google Book Search™ Service *(cont.)*

Where is Google Book Search service?

Google search term:
Google Book Search [or point your browser to **http://books.google.com**]
Advanced Book Search
http://books.google.com/advanced_book_search

Google Book Help Center
http://books.google.com/support/

Inside Google Book Search Blog
http://booksearch.blogspot.com/

Who should use Google Book Search service?

Any student or educator who is just beginning research on a topic can make good use of searching through some titles in print prior to physically going to the library to read the books. Not all books are available through Google Book search but those that are can be downloaded (if in the public domain), purchased through the bookseller links provided, or located in a library (local or distant).

Why should I use Google Book Search service?

Library use changes with each generation. Some important material is only available in book format and accessing the right material in print is often a daunting task for students. Using Google Book can help educators assess the content of a book for its relation to the topic, readability level, and to teach students about public domain materials and copyright laws.

When is Google Book Search service most useful?

The titles of Google Books Search service that you are working with can be saved in a feature called "My Library." To save the titles you would like to return to, log into your Google Account, search or browse for a title, and locate the "Add to My Library" link. You can access your library with the "My Library" link at the top of the Google Book page. This is useful for times when you cannot fully finish working with a book in the time period allotted.

Search Tools by Google *(cont.)*

Google™ Language Tools

What is Google Language Tools?

Google Language Tools is sometimes referred to as Google Translate because this tool will translate words, large amounts of text, and entire webpages from one language to another. Although there are many foreign-language learning software applications and webpages that provide translation, Google Language Tools is a valuable resource. Students may be interested in learning about Google's Language Tools because it appears as a link on the Basic Search page of Google. It is important to teach students that such translation tools are far from perfect and some caution needs to be exerted when using this tool in the classroom. A Google Account or Gmail™ webmail service is not needed to use Google Language Tools.

Windows and Macintosh users will need:
- Internet access and the use of a web browser (such as *Firefox* or *Internet Explorer*)
- Words or webpages in a language other than English

Where is Google Language Tools?

Google search term:
Google Language Tools [or point your browser to http://www.google.com/ language_tools]

Information about inaccurate translations
http://www.google.com/support/bin/answer.py?answer=32&topic=8997

"Livening Up Foreign Language" by Harry Grover Tuttle, Ed.D
http://www.techlearning.com/showArticle.php?articleID=196604811

Thank You in Many Languages
http://www.elite.net/~runner/jennifers/thankyou.htm

Who should use Google Language Tools?

Educators, students, and parents who have a need to translate a few words or sentences from one language to another or who need to view webpages in a language other than English should use Google Language Tools.

Search Tools by Google *(cont.)*

Google™ Language Tools *(cont.)*

Why should we use Google Language Tools?

Every minute of the day, webpages that are not written in English are posted by educators in other countries with exciting ideas for using educational technology in the classroom, but many teachers don't know they are there because they can't read them to access the information. With the global push in business, students will need foreign language skills more than ever before despite dwindling funds for cultural subjects. Awareness of other cultures is an important part of character education in classrooms of all grades.

Standards–Based Lesson: Gracias, Obrigada, and Merci!

MCREL Standards

Foreign Language: Standard 2: "Understands and interprets written and spoken language on diverse topics from diverse media": Grades 5-8: Level III, Benchmark 1 and 2 and Grades 9-12: Level IV, Benchmarks 2 and 6.

1. For teachers who are not subject-specific foreign language teachers who wish to connect to the curriculum, a focus on foreign language, world geography, and learning about culture can be an inviting adventure. Respect and understanding for those who do not speak English as a first language is an important part of the character education of elementary and middle school students. Knowing the parent or ancestral country of fellow classmates, what language is spoken there and where it is on the map sets the stage for global awareness in high school. Use the "Search Across Languages" feature of Google Language tools to translate important words like *hello*, *goodbye*, *happy birthday* and *thank you* in the languages offered. Use the website suggested extending the lesson to exploring *thank you* in languages not offered by Google.

2. The Google Language Tools search page lists the specific foreign languages that can be set on your Google homepage. Brainstorm with students how this would assist those whose English language skills are not accomplished enough to be able to read webpages except in their own language. Locate a webpage authored in a language other than English and use the single webpage translator to demonstrate the imperfect nature of language translation.

   - *Example:* Translate the University of Madrid's webpage at <**http://www.ucm.es/**> from Spanish to English to practice this skill.

Search Tools by Google *(cont.)*

Google News™ News Service

What is Google News™ news service?

Google News gathers together (aggregates) headlines from websites that offer news in English on a global basis. Currently, there are 4,500 news sources that contribute to Google News™ service, and the page update times are listed for students to see, promoting the concept of our rapidly changing world. Google News™ service offers a way to personalize these headlines with links to multiple sources on the same topic giving a wider perspective. Google News™ news service is available in other languages. Scroll down to the bottom of the page to view the list of these languages. Google News does not require a Google Account or Gmail™ webmail service for its basic use.

Windows and Macintosh users will need:
- Internet access and the use of a web browser (such as *Firefox* or *Internet Explorer*)

Where is Google News news service?

- Click on the "News" text link at the top left of Google's Main page

  Google search term:
  Google News [or point your browser to http://news.google.com]

  About Google News
  http://news.google.com/intl/en_us/about_google_news.html

  Google News Archive
  http://news.google.com/archivesearch

Who should use Google News news service?

Educators who use current events in the classroom as part of United States or world history need access to the latest information available. Although there are many websites that provide local, state, and regional news, Google News can give a broader focus to news topics. Students can then learn to personalize the page to narrow down the amount of information. Managing the vast amount of information that they witness daily is an important skill for students to learn.

Technology news and health news are topics of great interest in our twenty-first century classrooms. In a year where there is a Presidential election, Google News™ news service is of great value.

Search Tools by Google *(cont.)*

Google News™ News Service *(cont.)*

Why should we use Google News™ news service?

With television available in many classrooms, educators have found great use for news stories within the curriculum. But for focused research for individual or group projects, the news headlines available at Google News are less time-consuming and can be accessed by the student at the library, home, or computer lab.

The "Top Stories " sidebar lists the news by category (World, U.S., Business, Elections, Sci/Tech, Sports, Entertainment, Health, and Most Popular) for quick access to more stories available in these categories.

When is Google News™ news service most useful?

International news stories are very useful for those high-school and college students whose studies require knowledge of the news, economy, and culture of another country. To promote real-world proficiency in a particular language, foreign language teachers can use Google News with ease.

Google News Archive searches historical news of the past. It has its own page with special help for use. The time line feature of historic news is not to be missed. For example, students who are studying the yearly Iditarod Dog Sled Race that takes place in Alaska can use the keyword "iditarod" at the Google News Archive to see stories on the previous year's race. The Timeline link puts news in chronological order. Click on the year to see expanded new archive stories for just that year. There are links to the major websites for this commemorative event.

Google Reader™ Feed Reader

What is Google Reader™ feed reader?

Google Reader automatically checks for new content at websites that offer "feeds" attached to them. Feeds automatically send the content to the Google Reader page so that users do not have to visit and read individual webpages on a daily basis. Websites that offer these feeds might be those that contain constantly updated news items, blogs, or podcasts. This is often called *syndication*. You are simply asking for information to be pulled from the Web and sent directly to you so you don't have to go looking for it. It is a big time-saver!

Search Tools by Google *(cont.)*

Google Reader™ Feed Reader *(cont.)*

As a user or reader, you subscribe (for free) to these feeds through Google Reader, which manages and displays the content you want to view on a single page. If you find the content of one of these sites is not useful for you, you can unsubscribe to it. Feeds that are Atom- or RSS-based can be read by Google Reader.

There is a "gadget" you can add to your iGoogle page after you set up Google Reader, which is useful for reminding you to look at your subscriptions daily.

Windows and Macintosh users will need:

- Internet access and the use of a web browser (such as *Firefox* or *Internet Explorer*)

- Your Google Account

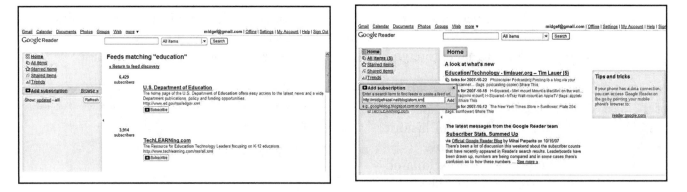

Where is Google Reader™ feed reader?

Google Search term:
Google Reader [or point your browser to **http://reader.google.com**]

Tour of Google Reader™ feed reader
http://www.google.com/intl/en/googlereader/tour.html

Google Reader™ feed reader Help Center
http://www.google.com/support/reader/

Search Tools by Google *(cont.)*

Google Reader™ Feed Reader *(cont.)*

Who should use Google Reader™ feed reader?

Educators who like to keep up with advancing trends in educational technology and education in general should use Google Reader to help them stay current without having to visit multiple sites. With their feed reader subscription, they can use any computer connected to the Web to access these sites. Educators interested in reading blogs on education or on another topic of interest will find Google Reader to be an invaluable tool.

Why should we use Google Reader™ feed reader?

Learning to use "feeds" (RSS readers) may be new to many educators, but will become necessary as there is more and more information to be accessed and managed on the Web. Daily reading of pertinent information via multiple websites is a time-consuming process and can be done more rapidly via Google Reader.

When is Google Reader™ feed reader most useful?

Google Reader is useful for those educators who are doing research as part of a graduate class, developing curriculum materials, or writing a thesis. High-school students doing research that involves the use of current trends only available on the Web will find that the use of Google Reader can help manage these tasks.

Getting Started with Google Reader™ Feed Reader

After signing in to your Google Account and taking the tour provided, you will be ready to set up Google Reader. You may find it helpful to browse through the Google Reader Help Center pages before beginning.

Google Reader offers collections of related feeds on a particular topic. In addition to education, news, sports, and technology are of interest to many teachers. In the Google Reader search box, type the keyword "education" to see feeds offered that are related to the fields of education. Explore these feeds until you locate the one for TechLearning.com, which is the blog for the Technology and Learning magazine.

Google Scholar™ Scholarly Texts Search

What is Google Scholar™ scholarly texts search?

Google Scholar is a search tool for scholarly papers, books, and dissertations. Using Google Scholar, educators and students can properly cite the sources and the narrowed searches performed that make evaluations more valid and easier to perform. A Google Account or Gmail service is not needed to use Google Scholar.

Search Tools by Google *(cont.)*

Google Scholar™ Scholarly Texts Search *(cont.)*

Windows and Macintosh users will need:

- Internet access and the use of a web browser (such as Firefox or Internet Explorer)

- Research topic or search term

Where is Google Scholar™ scholarly texts search?

Google search term:
Google Scholar [or point your browser to http://scholar.google.com]

About Google Scholar
http://scholar.google.com/intl/en/scholar/about.html

Google Scholar Help
http://scholar.google.com/intl/en/scholar/help.html

Advanced Scholar Help Tips
http://scholar.google.com/intl/en/scholar/refinesearch.html

Wes Fryer: Educational Research with Google Scholar
http://www.speedofcreativity.org/2007/10/27/educational-research-discoveries/

Cell Phones in Learning by Liz Kolb
http://cellphonesinlearning.wikispaces.com/

From Toy to Tool: Cell Phones in School by Liz Kolb
http://toytotool.blogspot.com/

"Using Cell Phones in Schools for Learning" by Marc Prensky
http://www.marcprensky.com/blog/archives/000043.html

Search Tools by Google *(cont.)*

Google Scholar™ Scholarly Texts Search *(cont.)*

Who should use Google Scholar™ scholarly texts search?

Any educator who is doing research should turn to Google Scholar to assist him or her with finding the right materials to read and study, rather than using Google's regular search procedure. Google Scholar finds current research papers and discussions that have been posted to the Web, plus the titles of books on the topic. Google Scholar is a full-text search tool and includes peer reviews of online journals along with the location of resources in print.

Why should we use Google Scholar™ scholarly texts search?

Students who are moving from high school to college need to learn new ways of finding the best resources available to them, and educators who are doctoral or master's candidates should be looking at both traditional print and Web resources as sources to be evaluated. Search results also include articles from related disciplines, such as uses of technology-related items in the fields of science and medicine, for a look at real-world application.

When Is Google Scholar™ scholarly texts search most useful?

Google Scholar is most useful for broadly searching scholarly topics, as the regular search methods will also provide hits of nonscholarly work, opinions, and webpages that may not be of interest to educators. Google Scholar can also search by the author's name and can include materials from conferences and lists of anthologies.

How Do I Use Google Scholar™ scholarly texts search?

There is both a Basic Search and an Advanced Search page in Google Scholar. For current articles for science and medicine, the Advanced Search page helps narrow down both the topic and the dates, and gives a list of broad subject areas. After working with the Basic Search page to locate the journals and books available, use the Advanced page to find more specific information or more work done by a particular author.

Search Tools by Google *(cont.)*

Google Scholar™ Scholarly Texts Search *(cont.)*

Standards–Based Lesson: Cell Phones and Education

MCREL Standards

Technology: Standard 3: "Understands the relationships among science, technology, society, and the individual": Grades 6-8: Level III, Benchmark 5 and Grades 9-12 Level IV, Benchmark 5.

1. On the basic search page of Google Scholar, enter the following search terms: "cell phones" and "education." When you examine the results, you will see that there are almost 50, 000 found. Since this is a hot topic in education, only current work would be useful.

2. Click on the link for "Recent articles." Notice that this cuts the amount of resulting hits by more than half so that the results that are relevant to cell phone use in the classroom are easier to locate.

3. Because Google Scholar offers a way to create a citation, it is important to look at the "Cited by" number before viewing the results of the hit.

4. Look through the list until you locate a journal article of relevance to education. Click on the link. Most likely you will be presented with the title of an article, the publication and date it appeared, and an abstract of it. Many journals are subscription-only, so it will be necessary to see if your local library, college, or university offers you access to this publication. Be sure to look through several pages of results as you may find an Adobe Reader version that is easily accessible from your home or school computer.

Looking at the Land and Stars

The first thing you'll notice in this chapter is the absence of screenshots. Google doesn't allow published images of Google Earth or Google Maps because Google does not own the copyright to the images which comprise the content. If you would like to read more about this, please do the following:

Point your browser to:

Google Permissions
http://www.google.com/permissions/index.html

Google Maps™ Mapping Service

Someday soon, it will seem strange to see people unfolding and studying a paper map. We will assume that the map must be an interesting antique map of the location. We will wonder how people actually navigated in their car using it and how they managed to fold it up. Ask any student and he or she will tell you that everyone looks up and prints driving directions from the many mapping websites of the Internet. The hottest holiday gift in the past few years has been a GPS device that can be moved from car to car.

What will become of companies that make maps, globes, and atlases? Within the next few years, will cars come with standard GPS devices installed, as well as connections for digital music players? How are educators supposed to teach map skills in the 21st century? Are classroom wall maps, atlases, and globes of the World an old-fashioned oddity? Should schools not bother to purchase these items anymore? It is something to think about.

What is Google Maps™ mapping service?

Google Maps mapping service is an online tool that provides street maps, point-to-point driving directions, and a way to find business locations in many global cities. In addition to street map and terrain view, the satellite or aerial views give this service a dynamic look easily understood and accessed by anyone with an online connection.

Recently, Google has begun to offer "Street View" for many major cities in the United States. This view is a 360-degree panoramic street-level view captured by a camera mounted on a vehicle driving down the streets. Although the images are static and not in real-time, this is a first for any of the online mapping services. Look up your own city and experience this for yourself.

Google Maps is available for use on Web-based mobile phones, which is a good selling feature for those of us who are always lost!

Windows and Macintosh users will need:
- Internet access and the use of a web browser (such as *Firefox* or *Internet Explorer*)
- Map skills vocabulary

Looking at the Land and Stars *(cont.)*

Google Maps™ Mapping Service *(cont.)*

Where is Google Maps?

Google search term:
Google Maps [or point your browser to **http://maps.google.com**]

Google Maps Help Center
http://local.google.com/support/

Google Maps Tour (video based)
http://www.google.com/help/maps/tour/

Google Maps for Educators
http://www.google.com/educators/activities/Maps_JCescalante.pdf

Ideas for Using Google Maps in the Classroom

- Explore the neighborhood around your school

- Locate all the schools in your district

- Use the "Street View" of a major US City to study buildings and houses

- Locate a major monument (like Ellis Island or the Lincoln Memorial)

- Discuss the difference between terrain and satellite views.

Google Earth™

Google describes Google Earth as a way to "Explore the world from your computer." Google Earth is frequently mentioned in the news, on TV, and is featured in movies. It is an amazing experience that everyone should have, especially since it is a free product (with full-featured paid editions) that you download to your computer. It should be noted that almost everyone who explores this software application first looks for his or her own house, which demonstrates how we "earthlings" feel about our place in the Universe!

The latest version of Google Earth also allows you to view the sky from different locations on the planet. You can use Google Sky, which is part of Google Maps.

What is Google Earth™ mapping service?

Google Earth uses images from the satellites that are above our planet. The satellites send images back to us and provide us with the information used by GPS devices. Google Earth's images are NOT real-time, so if your school recently added an addition to the building, it won't show up for quite some time. The images are on the average between one-and-two years old.

Looking at the Land and Stars *(cont.)*

Google Earth™ Mapping Service *(cont.)*

You need to have a high speed Internet access and an up-to-date computer with certain kinds of graphics cards, RAM memory and hard drive space.

Windows and Macintosh users will need:
- high-speed Internet access and the use of a web browser (such as *Firefox* or *Internet Explorer*).
- certain computer requirements. (see the FAQs link below.)
- to download the Google Earth software application.
- curiosity about our planet.

Where is Google Earth?

Google search term:
Google Earth [or point your browser to **http://earth.google.com**]

Google Earth Review's Guide
http://www.google.com/press/guides/earth_overview.pdf

Google Earth FAQs
http://earth.google.com/intl/en/faq.html

Google Earth Tour
http://earth.google.com/tour/index.html

Google Earth Help
http://earth.google.com/support/

The Sightseer (monthly email newsletter)
http://earth.google.com/sightseer_signup.html

Google Earth User Guide
http://earth.google.com/userguide/v4/

Basic Google Earth Help

You will see on many websites that discuss Google Earth a reference to KMZ files. KMZ (.kmz) files are the format for saved Google Earth locations and tours. As long as you have Google Earth installed, you can use these predesigned KMZ files without having to know anything about making KMZ files. Not all of these files are for education and some many contain content inappropriate for school use so please screen them carefully before using them with students.

Looking at the Land and Stars *(cont.)*

Google Earth™ Mapping Service *(cont.)*

Locating Help

Getting Help before Starting with Google Earth
> To locate the Guides and print them out, point your browser to:
> Juicy Geography's Google Earth Blog: Guides
> **http://www.juicygeography.co.uk/blog/**

Getting to Google Help while you are using Google Earth:
1. Download Google Earth.
2. From the Help menu, choose User Guide.
3. Your browser will open with the current Google Help.

Getting Started with Google Earth

Navigation

After launching Google Earth, "hover" your mouse over the upper right side of the screen to view the navigation controls. These controls disappear when you move your mouse away, but will be displayed when you return the mouse to that area.

> Navigation and the 3D viewer
> **http://earth.google.com/userguide/v4/#navcontrols**

Searching

Locating Stonehenge using a coordinate:
- In the search panel, type the following latitude and longitude and click the Search button (which looks like a magnifying glass): 51 10 44N, 1 49 34W

Locating Stonehenge using a keyword:
- In the search panel, type the word "Stonehenge" and click the Search button (which looks like a magnifying glass).

When you click the search button, Google Earth will fly to that location.

Placemarks

1. Search for a location and have Google Earth fly there.
2. On the toolbar, click the "Add Placemark" icon (which looks like a yellow pushpin)
3. A "New Placemark" box opens.
4. In the Name field, type a name for this location, and note the latitude and longitude.
5. With the "New Placemark" box open, drag the placemark to reposition it. Don't close this folder before you try to move the placemark.
6. In the Description box, type notes about the location or directions for students, then click OK.
7. If you wish to save placemarks when you exit Google Earth, be sure to answer *yes* when asked.

Looking at the Land and Stars *(cont.)*

Google Earth™ Mapping Service *(cont.)*

Making a KMZ file

1. In the Places panel, click on the Placemark or folder of Placemarks you created. When you click upon a placemark, this action selects it, making it ready to be saved.
2. From the File menu, choose Save, then Save Place as.
3. Navigate to a location on your hard drive, name the file, and click Save.
4. These saved files can be emailed to yourself or another person.

Using a KMZ file

Taking a Tour
http://earth.google.com/userguide/v4/ug_touringplaces.html

Tours are groups of saved placemarks. When you select a folder and then click the tour button, the tour will fly from placemark to placemark in the order they appear in the folder.

Add Content from a Gallery

Content in the form of saved KMZ files is available. In the Places panel, click the large "Add Content" button, which opens your browser and shows a gallery of KMZ files. Click Open in Google Earth to play the tour. (Remember to screen these before using them with students.)

Google Earth Lessons and Ideas

Innovative educators and travel enthusiasts have created placemarks and tours for you to use in the classroom, complete with lesson plans. Many of them have placemarks which, when opened, display photos of the area.

Learning About Asia

Although this page of resources was created for Geography Awareness Week in 2007, there are great ideas on how teachers can use Google Earth to teach about Asia in this combination project with National Geographic. Don't miss the helpful hints for new users of Google Earth on how to use KMZ files.

Google Geography Awareness Page
http://www.google.com/educators/gaw2007.html

My Wonderful World
http://www.mywonderfulworld.org/continents/asia/

Geography and Literature

Educator Jerome Burg has created an amazing resource for using Google Earth and literature. Click on the "Getting Started" link to read about how this resource can be used with your students. The video-based tutorials are a quick way to become comfortable with Google Earth. The Lit Trips are available for classrooms K–5, 6–8, 9–12, and higher education, and are growing in number. Teachers can create their own literature-based trips also, so be sure to read the information in the "Downloads, etc." section.

Looking at the Land and Stars *(cont.)*

Google Earth™ Mapping Service *(cont.)*

Google Lit Trips

http://www.googlelittrips.com/

Geography and the Last Great Race

Every year, Alaska is host to a special race to commemorate the 1925 delivery of diphtheria toxin to the Alaskan children. All over the world, educators follow this race as a special classroom project which encompasses character education, geography, literature, and math. Daily updates, now brought to us via the Internet, have enhanced this project and made it more exciting for students. To find tours for Google Earth, do a search on keywords "Google Earth" and "Iditarod."

Google Earth and the Iditarod Trail

http://www.earthslot.org/iditarod/index.php

Google Sky™ Program and Google Sky Maps

The ancient people depended on the stars and our moon for direction and sometimes evidence of the Creator. They were both fearful and in awe of our night sky. As you move to a location in Google Earth, you can switch to Google Sky and take a look at what you would see if you looked upwards from that spot (your current location) on our planet. You can also tour images from the Hubble telescope and examine the Planets in our Solar System. It's amazing!

A KMZ gallery of location-specific spots of the heavens and the planets are available for Google Sky just as they are for Google Earth. The animation of the Crab Nebula, which is over 6000 light years away, is not something you see every day. Using Google Sky is an important part of any planet or astronomy unit.

Google Sky was once only available through the downloadable application Google Earth but recently, Google Sky was released as a Google Maps option. This makes the Google Tool more appropriate for classroom use as it doesn't require any installation.

Windows and Macintosh users will need:

- high-speed Internet access (for using Google Sky with Google Earth) and a web browser (*Firefox* or *Internet Explorer)*; or Internet access and the use of a web browser (for Google Sky Maps).
- to download the Google Earth software application or use Google Sky Maps in your browser.
- curiosity about our planet and the heavens.

Where is Google Sky?

Google search term:

Google Sky [or point your browser to: http://www.google.com/sky/]

About Google Sky

http://www.google.com/sky/about.html

Google Sky Tour (for users of Google Earth and Sky)

http://earth.google.com/sky/skyedu.html

Looking at the Land and Stars *(cont.)*

Google Sky™ Program and Google Sky Maps *(cont.)*

What are Google Sky Maps?

With the release of Google Sky Maps, more users can experience the planets, historical maps, and view effects like infrared and microwave. Of interest to educators is the "Backyard Astronomy" option, which includes information about each selected object in the sky.

Google Moon

To commemorate the first lunar landing on our moon in 1969, Google has created a special extension of Google Earth and Google Sky that helps us better understand our own moon and the efforts made since that year to understand it. The six missions of the Apollo Missions are represented by placemarks and bubbles of information about the landings and the crews. Google Moon is not part of Google Earth, so you don't need to have Google Earth installed. For a look at the surface of the Moon, click the charts button and then the topographic tab. You will be surprised at how different the surface appears in different locations, but it is not made of green cheese as theorized!

Google Moon was created with public domain images of our moon and is part of Google Maps.

Windows and Macintosh users will need:
- Internet access and the use of a web browser (such as Firefox or Internet Explorer).
- curiosity about our moon and our space missions.

Where is Google Moon?

Google search term:
Google Moon [or point your browser to: **http://www.google.com/moon/**]

About Google Moon
http://www.google.com/moon/about.html

Google Moon Help
http://www.google.com/help/faq_moon.html

Useful Online Google Tools

Educators were disconnected from the online universe until schools began to offer a stable connection to the Internet in the classroom, computer lab, or library media center. These tools created by Google are meant to be used while online. Some of them are for creating products like word processing documents, spreadsheets, presentations, and webpages. Applications for these products are found in most schools, colleges, and homes.

You should check to make sure that the content-filtering at your school location allows access to and use of these tools, though you will find them useful for professional and personal productivity at home even if they are blocked at school. And don't forget—they are free!

Google Notebook™ Tool*

What is Google Notebook?

Google™ Notebook is an online tool that you use to gather information from the Web. Web addresses (links or URLs), clippings of text from webpages, images, graphics, and photographs can be gathered into Google Notebook. You can even type your own text right into a notebook, and it will be stored along with the items you have gathered.

Your Google Notebook can be accessed from any location or any computer. All you need is a computer with a browser, an Internet connection, and your Google account. You can create more than one notebook.

You can share your notebook with anyone you chose to collaborate with, publish it by making it a public webpage, or keep it private. You can search for other publicly available Google Notebooks. Google Notebook is a graduate of Google Labs and is fully functional.

Windows and Macintosh users will need:
- Internet access and the use of a web browser (such as *Firefox* or *Explorer*)
- a Google Account

Where is Google Notebook?

Google search term:
Google Notebook [or point your browser to **http://google.com/notebook**]

Google Notebook Tour (a quick three screen tour)
http://www.google.com/googlenotebook/tour1.html

Google Notebook FAQ:
http://google.com/googlenotebook/faq.html

Google Notebook for Educators Information and Ideas
http://www.google.com/educators/p_notebook.html

*See "Google Changes" on page 80 for more information about Google Notebook.

Useful Online Google Tools *(cont.)*

Google Notebook™ Tool *(cont.)*

Who should use Google Notebook?

Anyone who is working on a project can use Google Notebook to help them organize the massive amount of information needed. Curriculum developers can use it to point faculty to resources that meet specific benchmarks by gathering the URL and clipping of text directly in one shared notebook. Teachers can share successful practices, idea, tips, and lessons to create a useful collaborative curriculum resource.

Preservice and in-service teachers who are taking classes through higher education will find Google Notebook useful for their group or individual projects and for developing lesson plans.

Students can set up Google Notebooks at school and then access their research from computers in the school library media center, public library, or at home.

Why should I use Google Notebook?

It used to be enough just to keep links to webpages as bookmarks. As the Internet has become a place of more than just text and a few images, a need has arisen for deeper organization. Keeping track of where he or she obtained information is a challenge for any student. With the enthusiasm of working on a new project, anyone (even an educator) can forget where and when he or she found that perfect source, graphic, photograph, or music clip. Google Notebook can also make learning citation easier.

When is Google Notebook most useful?

In addition to keeping your Internet research organized, Google Notebook can help when you wish to create a short lesson with links. You can share the information with selected users you invite to view it, or "publish" it to make it public for the whole world to see. It is faster than creating a webpage and can contain linked text for easy clicking. Use this as a professional development class idea with your fellow faculty and staff members.

> Google Notebook, Google Reader and Firefox by Wes Fryer
> [Point your browser to **http://tinyurl.com/2vz4zv**]

Getting Started with Google Notebook

To use a Google Notebook you must be signed in to your Google Account. Take the suggested tour of Google Notebook and look at the frequently asked questions (FAQs).

Download the Google Notebook Extension and then restart your browser. The Google Notebook icon will appear in the lower-right corner of your browser window. Click on this to create a new Google Notebook. At anytime, after installing the Google Notebook Extension, you can open any of your notebooks by clicking on that icon.

Useful Online Google Tools *(cont.)*

Google Notebook™ Tool *(cont.)*

While you are viewing webpages, you can add "clippings" to your notebook. Clippings might be text, links, or images. Right-click (Windows) or control-click (Mac) on the item, and from the menu that appears, choose "Note This" to send it to your Google Notebook. In many cases, it is best to select the text or image first before accessing "Note this" from the menu. Remember, you can have more than one Google Notebook!

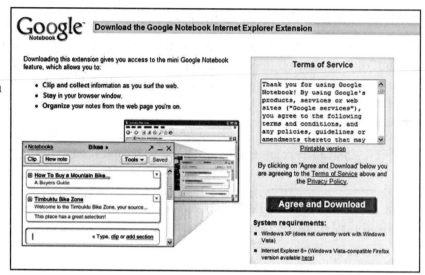

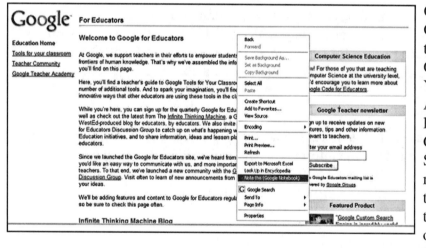

Once you have the items in your Google Notebook, you can organize them by choosing to view your Google Notebook in full-page view. You can do this from your Google Accounts page or by choosing the link "open in full page" from the Google Notebook extension. Sections can be added, moved, and renamed in this view. You can even type notes. Use the information in the Google Notebook FAQs to find out further information on using Google Notebook.

Useful Online Google Tools *(cont.)*

Google Notebook™ Tool *(cont.)*

Standards Based Lesson: Shedding Light on the Topic

MCREL Standards

Science: Standard 9: "Understands the source and properties of energy": Grades 3-5: Level II, Benchmark 4, and Grades 6-8: Level III, Benchmarks 4, 6, 8 and Grades 9-12: Level IV: Benchmark 4.

As part of a science unit, your students need to explore and gather basic information about light. Have the students begin to gather and evaluate Internet resources on light and place their links in a Google Notebook to review as part of the class project. Once students feel comfortable creating and managing Google Notebooks, you can move on to making this notebook as a shared or collaborative classroom project.

1. Guided by your curriculum and grade level, explore some websites on the properties of light with your students. Point your browser to these links to begin:

   There's More to Light Than Meets the Eye
   http://www.astrosociety.org/education/publications/tnl/35/35.html

   Measuring the Speed of Light
   http://www.colorado.edu/physics/2000/waves_particles/lightspeed_evidence.html

   The Science of Light
   http://www.learner.org/teacherslab/science/light/index.html

2. Ask students to share their thoughts on the importance of light in human life through an exploration of everyday expressions about light. (e.g. Light-hearted, light-headed, light weight, shedding light and bring secrets to light) Can students think of additional expressions about light, dark, and shadows?

3. As part of a unit on good health, have students investigate the relationship between the amount of light, seasonal affect disorder (SAD), depression, and addiction. With low levels of winter light in many areas of the globe in the winter months, mental and physical problems are common for those who live there.

   Seasonal Affect Disorder (Mayo Clinic)
   http://www.mayoclinic.com/health/seasonal-affective-disorder/DS00195

Google Docs™ Program

What is Google Docs?

Google Docs is an online group of tools for working with word processing, spreadsheets and presentation documents. It is useful for importing existing documents created by desktop applications or for creating new documents. Google Docs allows users to share or collaborate on documents, which many teachers find useful for lessons that require peer editing. All word processing documents, spreadsheets, and presentations can be used for individual, paired, small-group, or whole-class work.

Useful Online Google Tools *(cont.)*

Google Docs™ Program *(cont.)*

Windows and Macintosh users will need:

- Internet access and the use of a web browser (such as *Firefox* or *Internet Explorer*)

- a Google Account or a Gmail account

- previously created word processing, spreadsheet, or presentation documents or assignments for new documents

- photographs (for presentations)

Where is Google Docs?

Google search term:
Google Docs [or point your browser to http://docs.google.com]

Google Docs for Education
http://www.google.com/educators/p_docs.html

Online Tour
http://www.google.com/google-d-s/tour1.html

Google Docs Help Center
http://docs.google.com/support

Microsoft®'s Lesson Plans for Students and Teachers
http://www.microsoft.com/Education/LessonPlans.mspx

Brush with History: Google Docs
http://groups.google.com/group/brushwithhistory

Docs & Spreadsheets in the Classroom by Esther Wojcicki, Teacher
http://www.google.com/educators/learning_materials/necc_docs_spreadsheets.pdf

Who should use Google Docs?

Any teacher who is presently using a word processing, spreadsheet, or presentation software application and has a connection to the Internet can use Google Docs either in conjunction with, or instead of, desktop applications. Many of the features of Google Docs are much like those in the applications that you and your students have previously used. This makes the learning curve shorter so that you can focus on the curriculum needs of your class.

For a basic understanding of how Google Docs works, watch an online video called "Google Docs in Plain English" [point your browser to **http://blip.tv/file/384410**].

Useful Online Google Tools *(cont.)*

Google Docs™ Program *(cont.)*

Why should we use Google Docs?

Word processing documents, spreadsheets, and multimedia presentations are basic tools of technology used daily in both education and business. Students need to know the basics of these tools in their many forms as they are considered to be life skills. These tools are adaptable to many areas of the curriculum and all teachers should be using them in their classrooms. Having them available online for free is one of the benefits of using Google in education.

When is Google Docs most useful?

Google Docs is most useful for students who do not have the same type of word processing, spreadsheet, or presentation software (or the same version) on their home computers that are on the school computers. Software applications like these are expensive and don't come preinstalled at computer purchase. Students who don't have a computer at home can access their work at any location that has online access, such as the public or school library, or at a friend's or relative's house.

All Google Docs documents, whether word processing, spreadsheet, or presentation, are automatically saved while the teacher or student is working. This is a huge advantage when working with younger students or when students are working in a location away from the teacher.

How do I use Google Docs?

After logging into your Google Account, you can access Google Docs from the text link at the top right of Google's Basic search page which reads "My Account." After clicking on that link, locate the link "Docs" in the list to access your saved work.

> Download and read this Google Docs "crib sheet" for teachers
> **http://www.google.com/educators/activities/pdfs_GTA/CribSheet.Docs3.pdf**

If you are working with one or just a few computers in a classroom with students who have their own Google Accounts, you will most likely need to remind the students to make sure that they log in when they begin their work and log out when they finish their work. This process of logging in and out may need monitoring by teachers until students become accustomed to finding their own work.

Useful Online Google Tools *(cont.)*

Google Docs™ Program *(cont.)*

After you create or upload documents, you can edit them at the basic Google Docs screen. Below, as screenshots, are examples of each of the three types of docs available in Google Docs so that readers may see the work and the tools to create them.

Google Docs: Word Processing

Google Docs: Spreadsheet

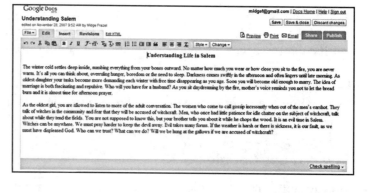

Google Docs: Presentation

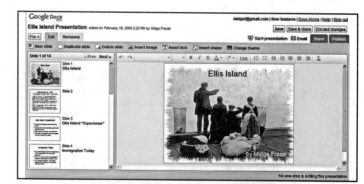

Useful Online Google Tools *(cont.)*

Google Docs™ Program *(cont.)*

Standards–Based Lesson: Buddy Writing with Google Docs

MCREL Standards

Technology: Standard 2: "Knows the characteristics and uses of computer software programs": Grades 3-5: Level II, Benchmark 1.

Technology: Standard 2: "Uses the advanced features and utilities of word processors": Grades 6-8: Level III: Benchmark 1.

Technology: Standard 2: "Knows the common features and uses of spreadsheets": Grades 6-8, Level III: Benchmark 3 and 4.

Business Education: Standard 22: "Knows the characteristics and uses of industry- and subject-specific computer software programs" Grades 9-12: Level IV: Benchmark 4 and Standard 22: "Uses presentation and multimedia software to design, create, edit, and format presentations": Grades 9-12: Level IV: Benchmark 3.

Business Education: Standard 4: "Understands and uses accounting software and spreadsheets": Grades 9-12: Level IV: Benchmark 1, 2 and 4.

Business Education: Standard 25: "Understands the acquisition of information systems: emerging technologies": Grades 9-12: Level IV: Benchmark 1.

Buddy Writing (Documents)
http://www.google.com/educators/weeklyreader.html

In keeping with promoting collaborative ideas in the classroom, Google Education has partnered with Weekly Reader to offer a free, online "buddy writing" [collaborative revision] lesson called "With a Little Help from my Friends."

Offered is an excellent step-by-step tutorial useful for any teacher to use to learn how to use Google Docs plus another document to aid in mastery of the revision features. These are "must-haves" for educators to read before working with buddy writing.

Picasa™ Photo Organizing Software

What is Picasa?

Picasa™ is a free downloadable application from Google™ for Windows users that, when installed, automatically scans your computer for images and videos that have been stored on your hard drive. (Macintosh users have the option of using Picasa Web Albums.) Picasa creates an organized library of "found media;" plus it offers tools for manipulating, renaming, and sharing those images and movies. Picasa offers the most common of graphics manipulating tools such a cropping, straightening, red-eye reduction, sharpening, lighting adjustment and tools for quick brightness/contrast and color fix. Special effects are available such as converting photographs to sepia tone or black and white, or to add a glow or grainy film appearance. You can make a collage from multiple photos, send your photos to your Google Blog weblog, or make a movie from still photographs. A great time-saving feature is the ability to quickly save altered images to a USB storage flash drive or burn them to a CD for backup.

Useful Online Google Tools (cont.)

Picasa™ Photo Organizing Software (cont.)

Windows and Macintosh users will need:

- Internet access and the use of a web browser (such as *Firefox* or *Internet Explorer*)
- the ability to download and install applications
- a Google Account

Where is Picasa?

Google search term:
Picasa [or point your browser to http://picasa.google.com]

Picasa Tour (a quick six screen tour)
http://picasa.google.com/features/index.html

Picasa Getting Started Guide
http://www.google.com/help/hc/images/picasa_user_guide.pdf

Picasa in the Classroom Educators Help Sheet
http://www.google.com/educators/activities/pdfs_GTA/CribSheet.Picasa3.pdf

Picasa Support and FAQs:
http://picasa.google.com/support/

Snooping Picasa
http://www.techlearning.com/showArticle.php?articleID=196604773

Who should use Picasa?

Picasa is only available for those users of Windows 2000, XP, and Vista. (There is an older version available for Windows 98). Macintosh users can use Picasa Web Albums if Internet access is available. See page 80 for more information about Picasa for Macintosh users.

Why should we use Picasa?

If you are an educator who needs help locating stored photographs and movie clips or has students who are working with digital photography, images, and movies in multimedia presentations or desktop publishing projects, then having them learn to use Picasa will save time with the design process plus provide file managements skills.

When is Picasa most useful?

Picasa is wonderful for those classroom situations where there is a need to organize and access graphics, photographs, or movies for use in curriculum projects. In a classroom setting, teachers can quickly locate and monitor any of these media. This will help to make teaching file management for project-based learning easier. Teachers working with multiple computers in a classroom or lab can easily delete unwanted photos or movies at the beginning or end of the year or when a unit or project is complete.

Useful Online Google Tools *(cont.)*

Picasa™ Photo Organizing Software *(cont.)*

Standards Based Lesson: Creating a Collage with Picasa

MCREL Standards

Language Arts: Standard 9: "Uses viewing skills and strategies to understand and interpret visual media": Grades 3-5: Level II, Benchmark 6:3 and Grades 6-8: Level III, Benchmark 6:2. Standard 10: "Understands the characteristics and components of the media": Grades 6-8: Level III, Benchmark 6:3.

Art Connections: Standard 3: "Uses critical and creative thinking in various arts and communications settings": Grades 9-12: Level IV: Benchmark 8:4.

Technology: Standard 2: "Knows the characteristics and uses of computer software programs": Grades 9-12: Level IV, Benchmark 4:1.

What is a Collage?

1. Have the students use Google search to define the word *collage*. Ask the students to decide which definition is appropriate for working with photographs.

   ("An artwork comprising of portions of various existing images such as from photographs or prints and arranged so that they join, overlap, or blend to create a new image.")

2. Physically demonstrate overlapping by using some previously printed photographs. Promote a classroom discussion of how television and print advertisements use overlapping or joined photographs to create a new image.

Making a Picture Pile:

Before working with students:

1. After the installation of Picasa and the automatic process of gathering media from the hard drive is complete, have four or five suitable images for the curriculum-related project available in a folder that Picasa has organized.

2. Instruct the students in the basics of how Picasa works, placing emphasis on the importance of file management. Be sure that the students are working with the photographs, you have selected for this example lesson. Students should be working with the "Effects" tab to alter the photographs with special effects, adding captions, and then saving these photographs.

Useful Online Google Tools *(cont.)*

Picasa™ Photo Organizing Software *(cont.)*

Standards Based Lesson: Creating a Collage with Picasa *(cont.)*

Student-Centered Lesson:

1. Select the folder containing the photographs to be used.

2. Pull down the Create menu and choose Picture Collage.

3. The "Make Collage" dialog box opens. In the "Type" drop-down box, choose Picture Pile. The photographs in the folder will automatically pile themselves.

4. The "Options" drop-down box offers black, white, or gray background colors. The Background picture option selects a photograph in that folder to be used as a background.

5. Ask the students to experiment with clicking in different locations on the pile of photographs. They may expect to be able to drag the photos around to rearrange them but this is not a feature currently offered. If Internet access is available and time permits, have the students click the Help button within this "Make Collage" dialog and explore the resulting webpage.

6. With each click, the pile is updated. In a reasonable amount of time, they should find a combination pile that they like. Explain the steps required to save and the location where you wish the photograph to be saved.

7. The collage has now been saved in a format that can be used with a word processing document or a presentation tool for a follow-up project or presentation.

Additional Instructions:

Directions for creating collages with Picasa are located on the Picasa Help page or by doing a basic Google search with the question "How do I create a collage in Picasa?"

Useful Online Google Tools *(cont.)*

Picasa™ Photo Organizing Software *(cont.)*

Standards Based Lesson: Creating a Collage with Picasa *(cont.)*

Sidebar(s):

Picasa Helpful Hint: Initial Picture Scan

Picasa gathers information about the location of stored media when you first launch it. This beginning process takes time and is best accomplished before students begin to work with this application. As part of the setup process, the user must make a decision about which areas of the hard drive to catalogue.

Picasa Helpful Hint: Turn off the Media Detector

Picasa will automatically inform you each time about photos stored on insertable devices. Every time you connect a camera via USB, use a memory card with your card reader, or insert a CD in your CD-ROM drive, Picasa will look for photos and movie files stored on them and will try to import them. To stop the Media Detector, open Picasa, pull down the Tools menu and choose Options. Under the General tab, uncheck the box next to "Automatically detect media (shows icon in the system tray)," and then click OK.

Picasa™ Web Albums

At this time, Picasa is an application that is available only for Windows users, but both Macintosh and Windows users can create albums with Picasa Web Albums. Depending on your curriculum needs, using photographs in your subject area can bring a sense of community to your student's lives.

What is Picasa Web Albums?

Think of this Google online application as a great way to upload your photographs to the Internet, organize them, and share them with others. One of the best features of online storage is that your precious photographs are safely backed up on the Internet just in case something goes wrong with your computer. Backing up is only truly appreciated when computer disasters occur!

When using Picasa Web Albums, you must read and agree to the "Terms and Conditions" stipulations by clicking on the "I Agree" button on the webpage. The process of uploading photos is easy and straightforward. To be fair, you must only use photos that you have taken ("that you own") for your albums.

Windows and Macintosh users will need:

- Internet access and the use of a web browser (such as *Firefox* or *Internet Explorer*)
- a digital camera or photographs taken by students and stored on a flash drive

Useful Online Google Tools *(cont.)*

Picasa™ Web Albums *(cont.)*

Where is Picasa Web Albums?

Google search term:
Picasa Web Albums [or point your browser to: http://picasaweb.google.com]

Picasa Web Albums Help
http://picasa.google.com/support/bin/topic.py?topic=8989

Picasa Web Albums Uploader Download Page
http://picasa.google.com/web/mac_tools.html

Web English Teacher: Photography
http://www.webenglishteacher.com/photo.html

Who should use Picasa Web Albums?

Educators who would like to have students work with digital photography and promote visual literacy in assigned projects can use Picasa Web Albums to upload and organize specific photographs for students to use.

Why should I use Picasa Web Albums?

Money for field trips outside of the classroom is often hard to obtain. Many local field trips that connect directly to the curriculum in all grades may not be available. Most school districts mandate that there be a curriculum plan or web that teachers have created to demonstrate how learning intersects with specific benchmarks. Involving parents in these special events can make the planning, organizing, and actual visit go more smoothly, and having photos of this day outside of the classroom walls can make the event special for all involved. Posting (uploading) these photos to a Picasa Web Album and sharing them either with the specific parents involved or publicly with the world is part of twenty-first century learning goals. Remember to take photos of children with their backs to the camera, showing their involvement with the activities but still promoting their privacy. Read your school district's Acceptable Use Policy (AUP) before posting photos to any website.

Picasa Web Albums for Windows users:

1. Windows users can use Picasa Web Albums in conjunction with the downloadable Picasa application. So first download Picasa to your computer.

2. Launch Picasa and select the photograph(s) to be uploaded.

3. Click the Web Album button, give your album a name, and decide on the privacy settings.

Useful Online Google Tools *(cont.)*

Picasa™ Web Albums *(cont.)*

Picasa Web Albums for Windows Users: *(cont.)*

4. When the upload process is complete, click View Online. You can add photos, delete photos, add captions, and make onscreen slideshows.

5. Alternately, you can just set up a Picasa Web album without using the downloadable Picasa application.

Picasa Web Albums for Macintosh Users:

1. Mac users can use either of the following methods for uploading photographs to a Web Album. The first is to use a plug-in for *iPhoto*®, and the second is to download a stand-alone application.

2. If you already have your photos in *iPhoto,* then you can download the plug-in which works directly with the *iPhoto* application. Follow the directions on the webpage listed under "Picasa Web Albums Exporter for iPhoto."

3. If you would rather download a separate application, then look for the directions on the webpage for "Picasa Web Albums Uploader."

Getting Started with Picasa Web Albums

After taking photographs with your digital camera, create a folder on your desktop and place the photos within this folder. This will make the uploading process a snap! After creating the Picasa Web album, you can burn the photos in this desktop album to a CD or DVD for backup purposes and then discard the photos on the desktop and on the storage card in your camera.

1. Sign in to your Google Account; from the "My Account" page, choose Picasa Web Album in the list on the right (or go directly to **http://picasa.google.com** and sign in). From here, you can upload your photos and then create albums of photos. Remember to read the information under "Settings" to decide who can view your photo albums.

2. Create a New Album (giving it a name and short description) and then upload photos into it. You do not need to put the location of the photos on a map as that is optional.

3. When the upload process is complete, add appropriate, short captions for your photos. These captions will appear both under each photo and in the slideshow that you can create with Picasa Web Albums. These captions can be changed later by using the "Edit Captions" button on each album's toolbar.

4. Within each album created, your photos can be organized with the "Organize" button on the toolbar. Photos uploaded taken at different times can be sorted by date or by filename. The directions for rearranging photos are on the right for easy manipulation. Photos can be deleted or moved to another album in this "Organize" view. Click the Done button to return to your album.

Useful Online Google Tools *(cont.)*

Picasa™ Web Albums *(cont.)*

Getting Started with Picasa Web Albums *(cont.)*

5. For a quick slideshow of all of the photos in this album, use the "Slideshow" button. If you have a class blog or website, there are directions at the main album page with the copy-and-paste code that you can use for putting your slideshow online.

6. The "Share Album" button on the toolbar is where you can send an email invitation to others to view your Picasa Web Album.

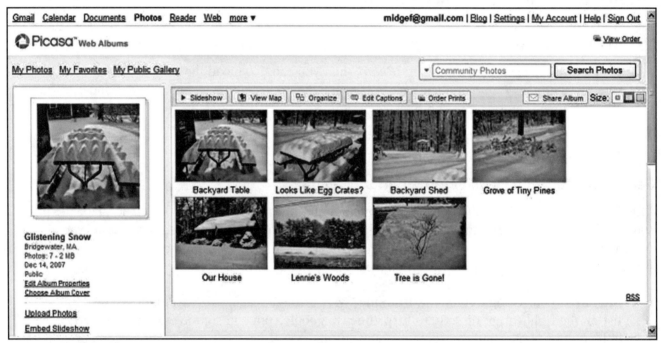

Standards Based Lesson: Beauty in Everyday Objects or Nature

MCREL Standards

Technology: Standard 2: "Knows and applies appropriate criteria to arts and communication products": Grades 9-12: Level IV, Benchmark 6

1. To promote visual literacy, teach digital photography skills. To teach students to apply criteria in judging artwork, direct them to take photographs that they consider to have a strong visual effect. These photos can be taken with the classroom digital camera inside or outside, on the school grounds, or in the city or town throughout the school year for an end-of-the-year culmination project.

2. Have students explore some photography websites gathered on the Photography page. This has been created by the Web English Teacher and is listed in the links in this section.

3. Brainstorm with students about how the attributes of everyday objects can be considered an art form, and develop a rubric for evaluating the photographs and the process of displaying them.

Useful Online Google Tools *(cont.)*

Picasa™ Web Albums *(cont.)*

Standards Based Lesson: Beauty in Everyday Objects or Nature *(cont.)*

4. Have the students submit the photos, upload them to a group or individual Picasa Web Album, and create their own captions. Have the students organize them by season, location, or date. Small-group peer-editing is a valuable skill for students to learn at this grade level.

5. Picasa Albums can be downloaded or submitted to a blog or website. Emphasize the importance of backing up photographs. Students may feel that photographs are so ubiquitous that they have little value for the future. It's worth discussing what *ephemeral* means to your students. Do the photographs have more meaning for students when gathered and used in a class blog, website, or presentation?

Path Through the Forest

Google Page Creator™ Tool*

What is Google Page Creator?

Google's Page Creator is an online webpage authoring tool. The webpages created are published and hosted on Google's servers, so you don't have to pay for Web hosting. Not all browsers are supported with this tool, and you'll need a Gmail account (and Google Account) to use this feature. Because this is an online tool, you must be connected to the Internet to create webpages (unlike software applications you purchase). An advantage of using Google's Page Creator online tool is that Google adds new features and improvements over time.

Windows and Macintosh users will need:
- Gmail™ webmail service and a Google Account
- Internet access and a web browser (*Internet Explorer 6.0* or *Firefox 1.0* or later) with JavaScript and cookies enabled
- photographs for webpages

*See "Google Changes" on page 80 for more information about Google Page Creator.

Useful Online Google Tools *(cont.)*

Google Page Creator™ Tool *(cont.)*

Where can I find Google Page Creator?

Google search term:
Google Page Creator [or point your browser to **http://pages.google.com**]

Learn About Google Page Creator
http://www.google.com/support/pages/

Google Page Creator Help
http://google.com/googlenotebook/faq.html

Google Page Creator in the Classroom
http://www.google.com/educators/activities/pdfs_GTA/CribSheet.PageCreator.pdf

Creating an ePortfolio with Google's Page Creator by Helen C. Barrett, Ph.D.
http://eportfolios.googlepages.com/howto

Who should use Google Page Creator?

Any educator or student can create webpages without purchasing webpage authoring applications by using Google Page Creator. Many educators have a requirement to create an eportfolio for their preservice or graduate studies work. Dr. Helen C. Barrett has created a webpage with ideas for using Google Page Creator for this purpose.

Those who wish to create a large website with many pages should not use Google Page Creator as there is a 100MB size restriction. Although the image uploading process is easy, because of the size restriction, it is suggested that the images be manipulated with a graphics application before they are uploaded.

The pages that you create with Google Page Creators are published with the following format. The words "yoursitename" listed below refer to the name you chose for your Gmail™ webmail service.

http://yoursitename.googlepages.com

Why should I use Google Page Creator?

Educators who wish to create a webpage or website (which is a group of webpages) can create one easily and quickly with Google Page Creator. Many teachers create a website to inform parents about classroom curriculum topics or to highlight special classroom events. Educators who wish to create webpage must read and comply with the Acceptable Use Policy (AUP) for their school or district before putting information about themselves or their students on the Internet.

Useful Online Google Tools *(cont.)*

Google Page Creator™ Tool *(cont.)*

Why should I use Google Page Creator? *(cont.)*

Students can learn to create webpages with Google Page Creator and, using the Site Setting Page, choose to "hide this site" from the Internet so that the pages do not get published. Webpages created can still be viewed by the classroom or computer lab teacher without the public seeing them. This meets the curriculum requirements without the worry of posting information to the Internet, but doesn't teach students about publishing their work and dealing with an audience.

Gmail™ Webmail Service

What is Gmail webmail service?

Even the most casual technology user uses email. Although Web 2.0 tools and text messaging on cell phones have made email take a back seat to newer forms of communication, email will be around for a long time because of its ease of use. Communication by email has changed how we look at the world, just as the invention of the telephone did for a generation long ago.

Google's email service is called "Gmail webmail service" ("Google-Mail"). It is a full featured, robust email application and is popular with teachers as they can access their email anywhere there is online access. With the popularity of Internet access on cell phones, (see "Gmail for Mobile Application" in the Help section of Gmail), your email can always be with you! Gmail has a very strong anti-SPAM filter, which is a welcome relief from unwanted communications. Gmail also has a chat component which some schools use as an inter-school messaging system to quickly and easily answer questions from people in the school or in the district. You can only chat with others who are invited and in your contact list.

Windows and Macintosh users will need:

- Internet access and the use of a web browser (such as *Firefox* or *Internet Explorer*)

- a Gmail account

Useful Online Google Tools *(cont.)*

Gmail™ Webmail Service *(cont.)*

Where is Gmail webmail service and how do I use it?

Click on the "Gmail" text link at the top left of Google's Main page to start the sign-up process and to read about Gmail

> Gmail's Help Center
> **http://mail.google.com/support/**

> Ten Reasons to use Gmail
> **http://mail.google.com/mail/help/intl/en/about.html**

Who should use Gmail webmail service?

Schools are one of the businesses whose employees ("teachers") use Gmail webmail service as part of the Google Apps program. Learn about how your school can use this effectively. Your administration should be made aware of this program for managing school communications.

If your school allows student access to Gmail webmail service accounts, they will have more possibilities to use many of the free Google applications described in this book.

> Google Apps for Education
> **http://www.google.com/a/help/intl/en/edu/index.html**

Why should we use Gmail webmail service?

Gmail webmail service can accept attachments that are up to 20 MB in size, which is larger than most email inboxes can accept. Virus scanning is automatic and Gmail webmail service blocks certain file types that are known to contain viruses. Gmail webmail service stores up to 2GB of your emails and gives you a readout at the bottom of the screen telling you how much space you have left before you must delete stored emails. You can import your email contacts from other applications or add contacts to your Gmail Contacts so that you can have the email addresses of your coworkers, family, and friends available to you from any online computer. The Help section of Gmail webmail service is excellent and easy to understand.

Useful Online Google Tools *(cont.)*

Google Talk™ Instant Messaging Service

Google Talk instant messaging service is an application that you download to enable you to chat by text and voice. Users can either chat using the Google Talk gadget or download the application to their desktops. Google Talk is part of the suite of tools called "Google Apps for Education." It is best used in a school environment as part of this Google program for schools. You can send files to another person using Google Talk instant messaging service.

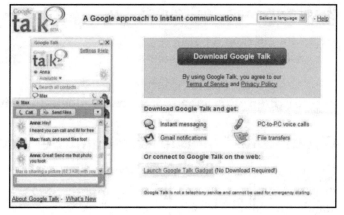

Windows and Macintosh users will need:

- Internet access and the use of a web browser (such as *Firefox* or *Internet Explorer*)

Where is Google Talk?

Google search term:
Google Talk [or point your browser to **http://www.google.com/talk/**]

Google Talk Help
http://www.google.com/support/talk/

Google Groups™ Usernet Discussion Forums

Google Groups Usernet discussion forums are discussion groups on just about any topic that you can imagine. Older technology-savvy teachers will remember that these types of discussion groups used to be called USENET. (Not all Google Groups Usernet discussion forums have discussions appropriate for education.) As mentioned in the beginning of this book, Google has several resources for teachers and this is one of them. Not all education happens in a school or just in the United States. The Internet is a great place for ideas in alternative forums for education, and many homeschoolers, religious educators, and teachers in schools in other countries have ideas to share from their educational perspectives.

You can create your own group for a specific learning goal such as the group created by educator Lucy Gray or join the specific group for educators who use Google in teaching and learning.

Windows and Macintosh users will need:

- Internet access and the use of a web browser (such as Firefox or Internet Explorer)
- A Google Account

Useful Online Google Tools *(cont.)*

Google Groups™ Usernet Discussion Forums *(cont.)*

Where are Google Groups?

Google search term:
Google Groups [or point your browser to: **http://groups.google.com**]

Google Groups for Educators
http://groups.google.com/group/google-for-educators

Google SMS™ Mobile Messaging Service

Google SMS mobile messaging service is part of a group of applications called Google Mobile. SMS stands for "Short Messaging Service." As cell phone technology has become part of our daily lives, it is inevitable that creative educational uses will be found for it. You don't need a cell phone to see how this works as there is an online simulation to show you what types of things you can do with text messaging. Cell phones are the biggest communication tools of the future.

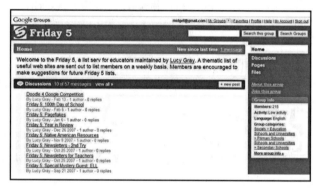

Windows and Macintosh users will need:

- Internet access and the use of a web browser (such as *Firefox* or *Internet Explorer*)

- a cell phone [practice first on the webpage with the phone facsimile]

Where is Google SMS mobile messaging service?

Google search term:
Google SMS [or point your browser to http://www.google.com/sms/]

Google SMS Help
http://www.google.com/support/mobile/bin/topic.py?topic=9123&hl=en

What is Google SMS mobile messaging service?

SMS is another term for text messaging. Most cell phones allow for text messaging, and many plans allow for so many text messages per month. To use this feature you must first investigate your cell phone plan to see if you have text messaging as part of your phone plan.

Useful Online Google Tools *(cont.)*

Google SMS™ Mobile Messaging Service *(cont.)*

How do I use Google SMS mobile messaging service?

Before using your cell phone for this feature, visit the Google SMS webpage and scroll down past the picture of a cell phone to look at the list of queries that you can ask Google. For example, you can find out the weather at this moment in Boston, Massachusetts. Instead of sending the query to a cell phone, type the words "weather boston" into the small search box on this page and then click the Send button.

The facsimile of the cell phone on this page shows you what you would see if you were sending this query from your cell phone to Google. Experiment with the search queries listed on this page before using the "Get Started Now" button at the top of the screen to set up Google on your cell phone.

Google sends a text message to your cell phone telling you to go to [point your browser to] **http:// mobile.google.com**. This text message will be from Google (466-453) which is GOOGL . This is how you test to make sure your text messaging works on your cell phone.

To use this feature without the facsimile on the Internet, you send a text message from your cell phone to Google with the query. In the example just given, here are the steps.

1. Start a new TXT message on your cell phone.

2. Send to 466453 (which will look like 466-453)

3. Erase any signature line you have set up.

4. Type: weather boston [or a big city near you] and send it.

5. You will receive a TXT message from Google with the weather.

Google Calendar™ Calendaring Service

What is Google Calendar™ calendaring service?

Google Calendar is a free online calendar that you can share with others. You can enter your medical appointments, birthday reminders, pick-up-the-dry-cleaning reminders, graduate-class-assignment reminders, and the dates and times of after-school activities, all the things that busy teachers have to juggle in a day's work. Needless to say, school schedules are hard to manage. There are important testing days, concerts, and field trips, parent-teacher conferences, and of course, school vacations and holidays. Life is a calendar event in this century, and teachers have more to manage than ever!

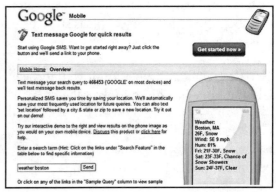

Useful Online Google Tools *(cont.)*

Google Calendar™ Calendaring Service *(cont.)*

Windows and Macintosh users will need:

- Internet access and the use of a web browser (such as Firefox or Internet Explorer)
- dates and names of personal or school activities and events
- a Google Account (or as part of Google Apps for Education)

Where is Google Calendar™ calendaring service?

Google search term:
Google Calendar [or point your browser to **http://calendar .google.com**]

Google Calendar Tour
http://www.google.com/intl/en/googlecalendar/tour.html

Google Calendar Help Center
http://www.google.com/support/calendar/

Nauset Regional School Student Activities Calendar
http://nausetschools.org/nrms/activitiescalendars.htm

Who should use Google Calendar™ calendaring service?

The advantage of having an online calendar is that it can be quickly updated and is accessible from any browser. Parents can use it to find out when school events are held. For an example of what a school can do with Google Calendar, you can view the calendar for the Nauset Regional Middle School Calendar in Cape Cod, Massachusetts.

How do I use Google Calendar™ calendaring service?

Calendar skills are a lifelong need, and your students can benefit from using Google Calendar to manage their assignment deadlines for each class. You can set up a calendar with important dates in history, birthdates of characters in literature, phases of the moon, and the birthdays of the class members (just first names, please). This classroom calendar can then be added as a "gadget" to the classroom iGoogle page.

Google Calendar has an intuitive interface, and it recognizes the words "tomorrow" or "next Tuesday" without your having to look at the date. There's even a "Quick Add" feature to enter events on the fly!

Click on the Settings link on the main Google Calendar page to find the option to share your calendar or create another calendar for your Google Account. All shared school calendars should have the permission of the administration.

Useful Online Google Tools *(cont.)*

Google Calendar™ Calendaring Service *(cont.)*

Standards-Based Lesson: It's a Date!

MCREL Standards

Historical Understanding: Standard 1: "Understands and knows how to analyze chronological relationships and patterns": Grades 3-5: Level II, Benchmark 1: Grades 6-8, Level III, Benchmark 3, and Grades 9-12: Level IV, Benchmark 4.

Mathematics: Standard 2: "Understands that mathematics has been helpful in practical ways for many centuries": Grades 3-5: Level II, Benchmark 1.

Calendars as Planning Tools

For planning lessons that revolve around dates on the calendar, these websites can be used as references by both teachers and students.

1. Use Google Calendar calendaring service to find the month in which you want to plan an activity. Click on the "Create Event" link. The New Event box opens and you can give the event a name, set a date or date range, plus store important information and a link in the Description box.

2. Using the event "Cinco de Mayo" (May 5) as an example, move to May and click the "Create Event" to open the New Event box. Enter the information, using the Description box to save the URLs of the planning resources. Then click the Save button. You will return to the calendar.

3. To find these planning website links again, click the event on the calendar and choose Edit Event Details. You can copy and paste a URL into your browser. This is a quick way to store a URL until you get to the classroom.

Lesson Planning Resources

Monthly Activities Calendar
(All kind of events by date)
http://www.enchantedlearning.com/activitycalendars/

Children and Young Adult Authors Birthdays
(Helps students find birthdays of their favorite authors)
http://school.discoveryeducation.com/schrockguide/authordate.html

Calendars Through the Ages
(Information about calendars)
http://webexhibits.org/calendars/

Through the Year
(Monthly activities)
http://server1.noblenet.org/nobweb/year/

Today in History
(Library of Congress daily list of historical events)
http://memory.loc.gov/ammem/today/today.html

Useful Online Google Tools *(cont.)*

Google Blog Search™ Service

Blogging in education is a relatively new way for educators, library-media specialists, and administrators to communicate new ideas with each other. The word "blog" is a combination of the word "web" and "log" as in an online journal or diary. People who blog on any topic of their choice are considered writers and publishers of their own work as they post their ideas, thoughts, and links with the world.

Readers of blogs usually read (or watch a video) and make comments. Some blogs are audio or video and are called "podcasts." Many blogs authored by teachers and consultants are on the topic of educational technology and are most easily found by using a list created by Kathy Schrock.

You can be a reader of blogs, a writer of blogs, or both. Many teachers are incorporating blog-writing in their lessons with students and are finding students to be highly motivated when they share their work with the world. It is important to teach students that blog authors may not be experts in their field and any blogs they read should be critically evaluated and facts verified.

Gmail webmail service or a Google Account are not needed to use Google Blog Search service.

Windows and Macintosh users will need:
- Internet access and the use of a web browser (such as *Firefox* or *Internet Explorer*)

Where is Google Blog Search service?

Google search term:
Google Blog Search [or point your browser to http://blogsearch.google.com]

About Google Blog Search
http://www.google.com/help/about_blogsearch.html

Advanced Google Blog Search
http://blogsearch.google.com/blogsearch/advanced_blog_search

Kathy Schrock's List of Education-Related Blogs
http://kathyschrock.net/edtechblogs.htm

When is Google Blog Search service most useful?

Google's Blog Search is most useful when you use its "Advanced Search" page. By using this page instead of the Google Blog Search service main page, you can better control what you are looking for. If you know that a friend has a blog, you can search for it by typing his or her name in the Blogs and Posts written by [insert name]. "Posts" are the individual entries written by those who blog (called "bloggers").

Useful Online Google Tools *(cont.)*

Google Blog Search™ Service *(cont.)*

When is Google Blog Search service most useful? *(cont.)*

If you are looking for a particular blog post that you read previously, you can search for it using the "Dates" search. And if you are a blogger yourself, you can see where you are mentioned in other people's blogs by typing your own name in the "Exact Phrase" search. Check the "About Google Blog Search" link for further information on this useful and interesting search tool.

Blogger™ Web Publishing Service

What is Blogger web publishing service?

Blogger™ web publishing service is a free online tool by Google that you can use to create a Google Blog™ weblog. As you learned in the Google Blog Search service section, blogging is a form of online writing. Creating a blog is different from creating a webpage in that you don't have to know how to write code or to know anything about Web publishing. In fact, the hardest part about blogging is deciding your goal or purpose for having one. Most educators start by reading blogs to get used to this new form of communication. Many teachers are creating classroom blogs when their schools allow this form of web publishing. If you are thinking about having your students learn to blog, you will need to make sure that Blogger web publishing service is not blocked by your school's content filtering rules. You may also be surprised to find out that many students already have blogs and know how to write one! Blogger web publishing service allows anyone to have more than one blog.

David Warlick of Landmarks for Schools is often quoted as saying that "blogging and podcasting are dramatically changing the landscape of global communication." Knowing about and participating in blogging is something every teacher should experience. (Warlick is the author of a book about classroom blogging and one of the leaders in the educational technology world.)

You could create a blog and then delete it just to see how it works, but hopefully you will find that you like blogging and will be encouraged by this online writing and communication tool. Bloggers (those who blog) must be encouraged to follow conventional tenants of good writing, be good citizens of the Internet, and learn to find their own voice in the "Blogosphere" (the world of online blogging) no matter their age or purpose for writing.

Windows and Macintosh users will need:
- Internet access and the use of a web browser (such as *Firefox* or *Internet Explorer*)
- Gmail webmail service and a Google Account
- a topic or subject of interest to blog about

Useful Online Google Tools *(cont.)*

Blogger™ Web Publishing Service *(cont.)*

Where is Blogger web publishing service?

Google search term:
Blogger [or point your browser to **http://www.blogger.com**]

Blogger Help Center
http://help.blogger.com/

David Warlick's Landmarks for Schools
http:// landmark-project.com/

Getting Started with Blogger

For most educators, deciding what they want to write about is the hardest part of blogging. Some graduate programs in educational technology include blogging as part of their curriculum in both face-to-face classes and online programs. Some educators use a blog to write about their hobbies or to pass along information to family and friends. In general, one person is the blog writer and others communicate by posting comments that the blog writer reads and responds to with another blog posting. You can also create a "team blog" in which other people are invited to post their writing to your blog. (See Team Blogging in the Blogger Help Center for more information.)

First, decide on a topic for your blog. Let's imagine you are going to write about Emerging Technologies in Education. Point your browser to Blogger's Main page and log in to your Blogger web publishing service account. Blogger web publishing service calls this "Step One."

The second step is where you have important decisions to make. In the box labeled "Blog Title," you will be typing what you want your blog to be called. This title will appear on the blog and in the title bar of your browser when people visit your blog. You will need an interesting, short, descriptive name. For the example we are using, we could name this blog "Emerging Technologies in Education." By the way, the Dashboard is the place where you will be returning to edit your postings, create another blog, or delete your blog. Yes, you can have more than one blog, but remember you should be a dedicated blogger and a frequent contributor to the blogosphere.

Useful Online Google Tools (cont.)

Blogger™ Web Publishing Service (cont.)

Getting Started with Blogger (cont.)

The next box will be the URL of your blog. Since Blogger web publishing service has been around a while, you will need to check what you type here in case someone else has already picked the same name that you would like to use. The URL of your blog will end in "blogspot.com" so a short name is best. In the third box, you must type the letters that appear on the screen. This is to ensure that you are a human and not trying to put unwanted messages in a blog. By the way, if you already have a website that you pay to host (not your school's website), then you can follow the instructions to have your blog associated with your website. Click the "Continue" arrow when this step is complete.

The third step is to choose a template for your blog. Blogger web publishing service offers many choices. Simple is always best and it is important to remember that simple also implies easiest to maintain. Think about your readers! Is this a pleasing color combination and is the text readable and easy on the eye? Don't agonize with this step as you *can* change it later. Once you are done with this step, Blogger web publishing service will set up your blog. You will be ready to post your first blog post. The interface at Blogger web publishing service is easy to figure out, and if you see something you don't understand, Blogger's Help Central offers clear explanations.

Some people blog daily, more than once a day, or just when they have something to say. The best way to decide what to write is to read blogs to see their appearance, what bloggers have to say, and how much is appropriate to write. Every time you visit Blogger's Main Page, you will be asked to log into your Google Account and then you will see your Dashboard.

From the Dashboard, you will see a list of your blogs. You can post (write) in your blog, view your blog, and create a new blog. In this example, we will write and post a new blog entry by clicking on the "New Post" link, which opens a new blog entry.

The blog-writing tools are held in the small toolbar that runs along the top of each blog entry area. Hover your mouse across the row to see the "tooltips" that appear, giving you an idea of the function of each button. The first few will be familiar, as they apply the font, size, color, and style attributes of your text. The next button allows you to add a hyperlink to text by typing or using the copy-and-paste method. Adding links to your blog posts is very important as it connects your readers to other blogs, books, webpages, and visual elements found on the Internet.

Useful Online Google Tools *(cont.)*

Blogger™ Web Publishing Service *(cont.)*

Getting Started with Blogger *(cont.)*

Text alignment is next, followed by numbering and bullet options. The checkmark with the symbol "ABC" on it is the spell-checker, which you should practice with, as it works a bit differently than the regular method used by your word processing program. It is important to mention here that you can write your blog entries in your word processing program and then copy and paste them into your blog entry.

At the far end is the eraser tool which removes any applied formatting that you may have applied and now don't want applied. The multimedia tools are in-between. They allow you to upload an image, a video, or a file to your blog entry. Many bloggers post their photos/videos to another location and "connect" them to their blog using the Web 2.0 idea of sharing across tools. It should also be noted that if you are knowledgeable with writing HTML code, you can switch to the "Edit HTML" area and enter your own code.

The labels section at the bottom allows the blogger to type a word or two to identify keywords of the post that he or she has written. These can appear at the end of the entry or in a link along the side of the blog. As an example, if you are writing about cell phones, you can label the entry with those words so that your visitors can quickly find the post. When your blog entry is complete, it is time to click the button "Publish Post." After that, all you need is an audience!

Google™ Custom Search

What is Google Custom Search?

Google Custom Search (previously called CSE or Custom Search Engine) is a Google Tool that allows you to create a customized search on a topic or keyword that you can use repeatedly to perform research.

Windows and Macintosh users will need:

- Internet access and the use of a web browser (such as *Firefox* or *Internet Explorer*)

- research topic or keyword

Where is Google Custom Search?

Google Search term:
Google CSE [or point your browser to **http://www.google.com/coop/cse/**]

Google Custom Search for Education
http://www.google.com/educators/p_cse.html

Useful Online Google Tools *(cont.)*

Google™ Custom Search *(cont.)*

Who should use Google Custom Search?

Google Custom Search is useful for both students and educators who are researching a topic on which there are too many webpages to focus a search. Older students can narrow down a topic using this tool and create several Google Custom Search engines for each member of a collaborative project.

Why should we use Google Custom Search?

In the younger grades, where students should be using teacher-identified links for their research, Google Custom Search makes it easy for the teacher (or team teachers) to decide which links the students must use to gather the information from websites. It is a timesaver for busy classrooms.

When is Google Custom Search most useful?

Google CSE is wonderful for students who are doing research in small groups or with a whole-class project in the middle-school years. As readability of text and content on webpages is an issue for many students, teachers can identify which websites are appropriate for the assignment.

How do I use Google Custom Search?

Download and read this Google CSE "crib sheet" for teachers
http://www.google.com/librariancenter/downloads/Custom_Search_85x11.pdf

Wilson Bentley and the Science of Snowflakes

Creator [Edit your profile]

Name: Mrs. Frazel
Member since: Sep 15, 2007

Contributors [Manage contributors]

There are no other users contributing at this time.

Search engine details [Edit this search engine]

Learn about the science of snowflakes through the life of Wilson "Snowflake" Bentley. Use these links to find information about how scientists study snowflakes as part of your unit on the water cycle.

searches 12 sites, including:
http://www.enchantedlearning.com/subjects/astronomy/planets/earth/Watercycle.shtml, http://ga.water.usgs.gov/edu/watercycle.html, http://www.kidzone.ws/water/, http://snowflakebentley.com/, http://snowflakebentley.com/snowflakes.htm

Keywords: "Snowflake Bentley" "Wilson Bentley" snow "caldecott medal" "water cycle"

Last updated: Oct 28, 2007
Add this search engine to your Google homepage [Google]
Add this search engine to your blog or webpage »

©2007 Google - Google Home - About Google - Privacy Policy

Useful Online Google Tools (cont.)

Standards–Based Lesson: Wilson Bentley and Snowflake Science

MCREL Standards

Science: Standard 1: "Understands atmospheric processes and the water cycle": Grades 3-5: Level II, Benchmark 1:1, 1:3, 1:9 and Grades 6-8 Level III, Benchmark 2:1. Standard 12: "Understands the nature of scientific inquiry": Grades 3-5 Level II, Benchmark 2:1, 2:2, 2:3. Standard 13: "Understands the scientific enterprise": Grades 3-5: Level II: Benchmark 1:1, 1:3 and Grades 6-8: Level III: Benchmark 1:1, 1:12.

Language Arts: Standard 7: "Uses reading skills and strategies to understand and interpret a variety of informational texts": Grades 3-5 Level II, Benchmark 1, 2 and Grades 6-8 Level III: Benchmark 4.

1. As part of a lesson on reading biographies, have students read a book about Wilson Bentley. Perform a Google Search with the term "Wilson Bentley" or use Google's Book Search to quickly locate a list of titles appropriate for your students. Older students may wish to examine a book written about him with photographs of his snowflake research. Check the public library for availability of these titles.

2. Examine the Google Custom Search Engine created for this lesson to find links to webpages for your students to combine learning about the water cycle and snowflake science. Your students may think it would be easy to photograph a snowflake! Point your browser to:

   http://tinyurl.com/2yqdje

3. Visit the webpage created for snowflake science from a real scientist at the California Institute of Technology. Point your browser to:

   http://www.its.caltech.edu/~atomic/snowcrystals/

4. Ideas for questions to extend this lesson:

   - How many areas of the United States do not experience snow at any time of the year?

   - What temperature range is conducive to snow and what is the difference between snow, ice, and rain?

Google™ for Educators

Google, knowing that educators are busy people, has neatly organized some useful resources for education in one area. For those teachers who enjoy keeping up with the current advances in educational technology, these webpages are easy to use and quick to access.

Windows and Macintosh users will need:

- Internet access and a web browser

- an email address (school, personal or Gmail webmail service)

- *Adobe Reader* (free) (.pdf)

Welcome to Google for Educators

Point your browser to:
http://www.google.com/educators/index.html

Your first task is to sign up for the email newsletter by entering your email address in the box in the section that reads "Google Teacher Newsletter."

The Google Teacher Community is a Google Group that you can join. You can join in the conversation and ask questions about any of the tools that you'd like to use in your classroom. Just sign up by entering your email address in the section that reads "Discussion Group."

Google Teacher Community

Point your browser to:
http://www.google.com/educators/community.html

This group offers a special section where you can view submitted lesson plans. Why not join the collaboration by working up one of your own lesson plans that uses a feature of Google? While you're thinking about that you can peruse the posts in the section "Google in Your Classroom" and see the questions, answers, and ideas presented there.

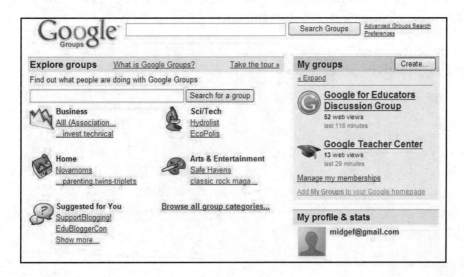

Google™ for Educators *(cont.)*

Google Teacher Community *(cont.)*

Another Google Group you can join is called the "Google Teacher Center." The past newsletters are archived so that you can see what you've been missing.

Google Teacher Center

Point your browser to:
http://groups.google.com/group/Google-Teacher-Center

Infinite Thinking Machine

The Infinite Thinking Machine, a blog sponsored by Google in conjunction with West Ed, is written by several contributors. In addition to discussion about 21st century educational technology ideas, it offers short video programs that you can watch in your browser through Google Video or view in Apple®'s iTunes. These videos are also downloadable in QuickTime™ format (.mov) for easy viewing offline in a professional development setting. Chris Walsh is the host of the video series. Check out the link to ITM7 as an example of this type of learning tool.

Point your browser to:
http://www.infinitethinking.org/

ITM7: Show and Tell
http://www.infinitethinking.org/2007/04/itm-7-show-tell.html

About WestEd
http://www.wested.org/cs/we/print/docs/we/home.htm

Google Teacher Academy

Want to attend a free, one-day professional development experience to help you get the most out of the new tools offered by the Internet? This special academy, whose attendance leads to becoming a Google Certified Teacher, is just getting started. Fifty teachers will be chosen by application to attend. If chosen, you must provide your own travel arrangements.

Point your browser to:
http://www.google.com/educators/gta.htm

Google™ for Educators *(cont.)*

Classroom Activities

Today's professional environment for educators has been moving toward a collaborative environment since education discovered the Internet as a medium for sharing teacher-created lessons, activities, and ideas. Peruse these offerings to get started using the tools offered by Google!

First Step: Read, Print and Share

Google Education Classroom Activities
Point your browser to (and access with Adobe Reader) these activities plus more:
http://www.google.com/educators/activities.html

- Google Search Tips

- Google Earth "crib sheet"

- Google Docs and Spreadsheets "crib sheet"

- Maps in the Classroom

- Blogger Basics

Second: Three Easy Steps

Cheryl Davis's "Gone Google": On the Go Lesson ideas
Point your browser to:
http://gctgone.googlepages.com/home

"A Place in Time"

Experience the impact of images on the learning of history using Google Tools.

1. Move to the page for "A Place in Time" by clicking on the link.

2. Watch the video in your browser or download it to your hard drive for offline viewing later.

3. Grab the lesson by clicking on its link, and then saving it to your hard drive or printing it out to share.

Classroom Posters

If you are longing for more freebies, take a look at the wonderful posters for your bulletin boards or classroom walls. You'll want to print them out (in color) and laminate them. Some are also in sizes to be used as handouts for your faculty meetings, professional development sessions, or graduate classes. These posters, along with the classroom activities will give your faculty ideas on how to use Google in your school. Did you notice them featured in the photograph in the Introduction to this book?

Google™ for Educators *(cont.)*

Classroom Posters *(cont.)*

Google Classroom Posters
http://www.google.com/educators/posters.html

Google Changes

Nothing endures but change.—Heraclitus

In the today's technological world, nothing stays the same. Since this book was written, changes have been made to some of Google's Tools.

Google has stopped development on Google Notebook, and new users can no longer start a Notebook. Current users will be still be able to access their Notebooks.

For more information, point your browser to:

Official Google Notebook Blog—Stopping Development on Google Notebook

http://googlenotebookblog.blogspot.com/2009/01/stopping-development-on-google-notebook.html

Macintosh users whose computers have Intel processors can now use Picasa software. Picasa has released a beta version for Macs.

For more information, point your browser to:

Picasa for Mac

http://picasa.google.com/mac/

Google Page Creator is no longer accepting new signups as Google is now focusing on Google Sites, which has more features and a more collaborative nature.

For more information, point your browser to:

Google Sites

http://sites.google.com/